# 75 GREAT STANDARDS

## Arranged by Richard Bradley

**Richard Bradley** is one of the world's best-known and best-selling arrangers of piano music for print. His success can be attributed to years of experience as a teacher and his understanding of students' and players' needs. His innovative piano methods for adults (*Bradley's How to Play Piano* – Adult Books 1, 2, and 3) and kids (*Bradley for Kids* – Red, Blue, and Green Series) not only teach the instrument, but they also teach musicanship each step of the way.

Originally from the Chicago area, Richard completed his undergraduate and graduate work at the Chicago Conservatory of Music and Roosevelt University. After college, Richard became a print arranger for Hansen Publications and later became music director of Columbia Pictures Publications. In 1977, he co-founded his own publishing company, Bradley Publications, which is now exclusively distributed worldwide by Warner Bros. Publications.

Richard is equally well known for his piano workshops, clinics, and teacher training seminars. He was a panelist for the first and second Keyboard Teachers' National Video Conferences, which were attended by more than 20,000 piano teachers throughout the United States.

The home video version of his adult teaching method, *How to Play Piano With Richard Bradley*, was nominated for an American Video Award as Best Music Instruction Video, and, with sales climbing each year since its release, it has brought thousands of adults to—or back to—piano lessons. Still, Richard advises, "The video can only get an adult started and show them what they can do. As they advance, all students need direct input from an accomplished teacher."

Additional Richard Bradley videos aimed at other than the beginning pianist include *How to Play Blues Piano* and *How to Play Jazz Piano*. As a frequent television talk show guest on the subject of music education, Richard's many appearances include "Hour Magazine" with Gary Collins, "The Today Show," and "Mother's Day" with former "Good Morning America" host Joan Lunden, as well as dozens of local shows.

Project Manager: Tony Esposito

2

**Contents:**

# OVER THE RAINBOW

From the Motion Picture *The Wizard of Oz*

Lyric by E.Y. HARBURG
Music by HAROLD ARLEN
*Arranged by Richard Bradley*

Over The Rainbow - 3 - 1

5

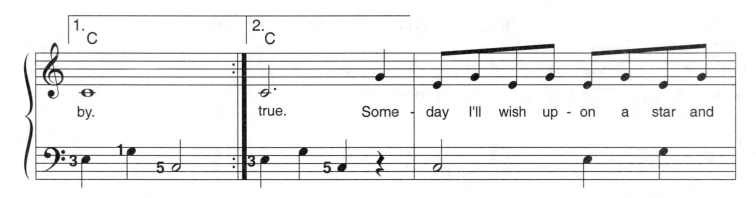

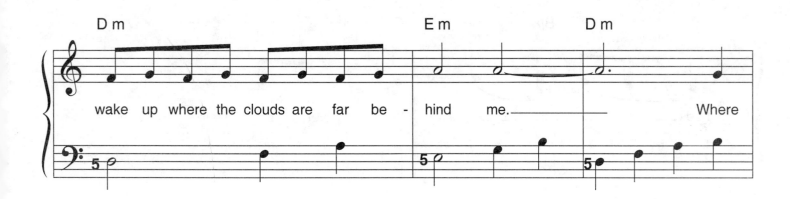

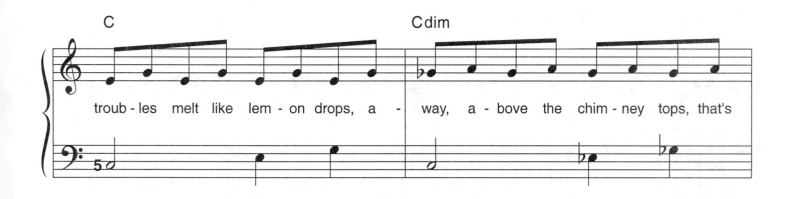

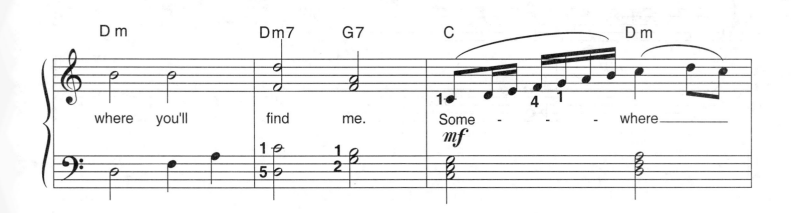

# WHAT A WONDERFUL WORLD

Words and Music by
GEORGE DAVID WEISS and BOB THIELE
*Arranged by Richard Bradley*

What A Wonderful World - 3 - 1

8

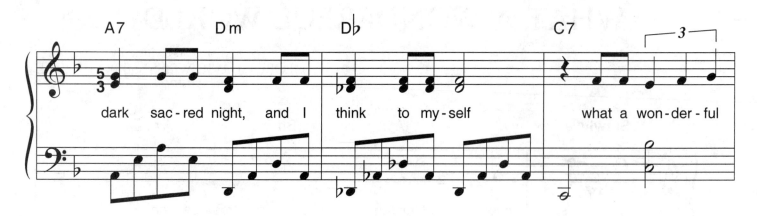

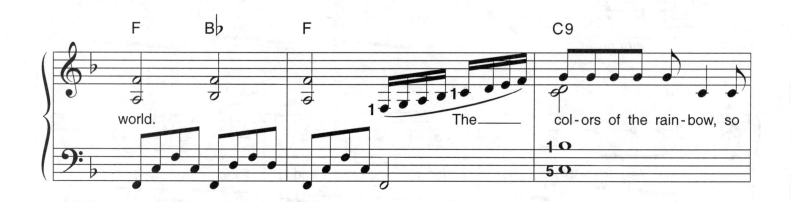

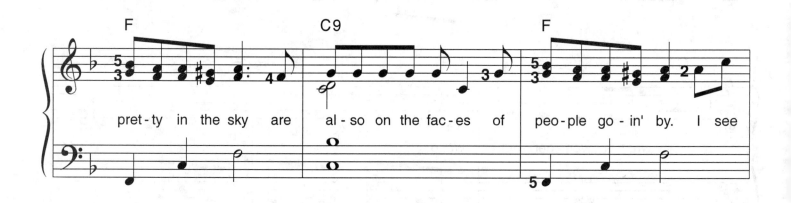

# AS TIME GOES BY

From the Motion Picture *Casablanca*

Words and Music by
HERMAN HUPFELD
*Arranged by Richard Bradley*

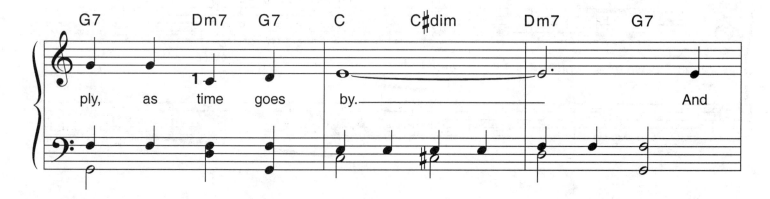

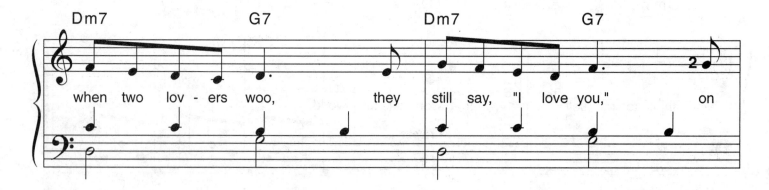

As Time Goes By - 4 - 1

that you can re - ly;\_\_\_\_\_ No mat - ter what the fu - ture

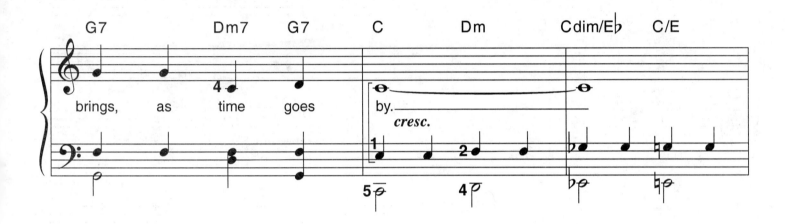

brings, as time goes by.\_\_\_\_\_
cresc.

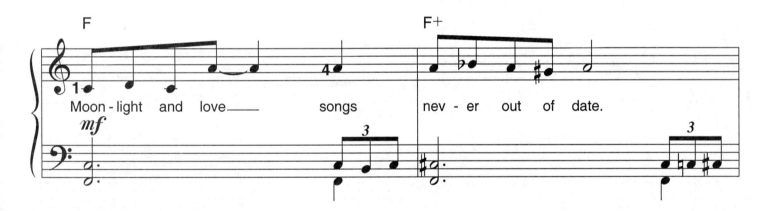

Moon - light and love\_\_\_ songs nev - er out of date.
mf

Hearts full of pas - sion, jeal - ous - y and hate;

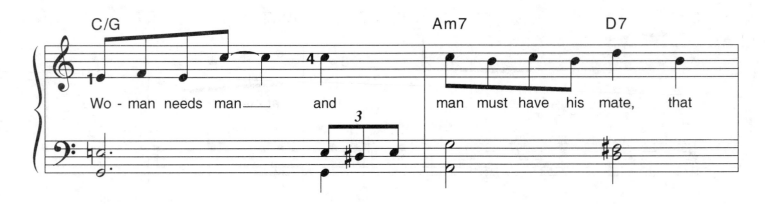

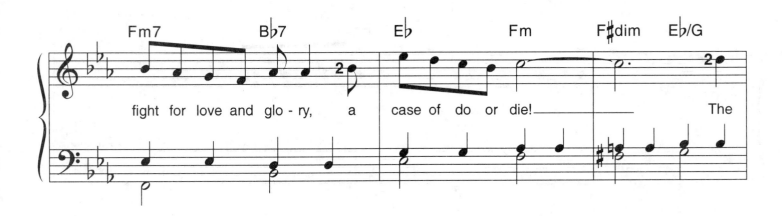

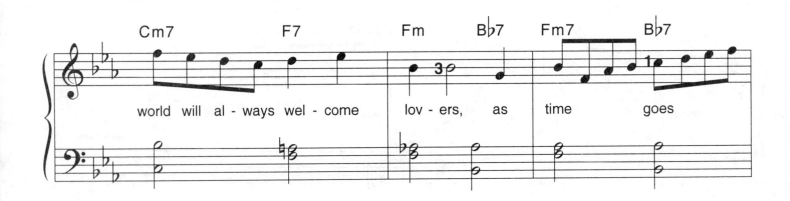

# MISTY

Lyric by
JOHNNY BURKE

Music by
ERROLL GARNER
*Arranged by Richard Bradley*

Misty - 3 - 1

Verse 3:
On my own, would I wander through this wonderland alone,
Never knowing my right foot from my left,
My hat from my glove, I'm too misty and too much in love.

# SOMEONE TO WATCH OVER ME

From the Broadway Musical *Oh, Kay!*

Words by IRA GERSHWIN
Music by GEORGE GERSHWIN
*Arranged by Richard Bradley*

Someone To Watch Over Me - 3 - 1

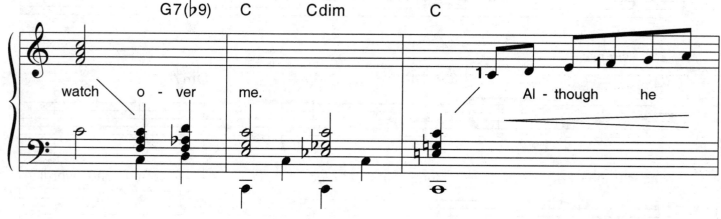

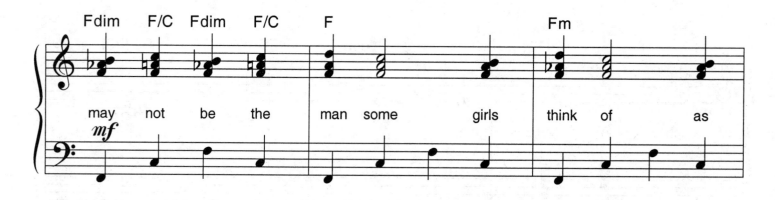

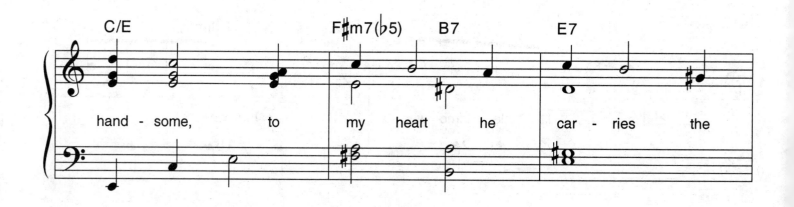

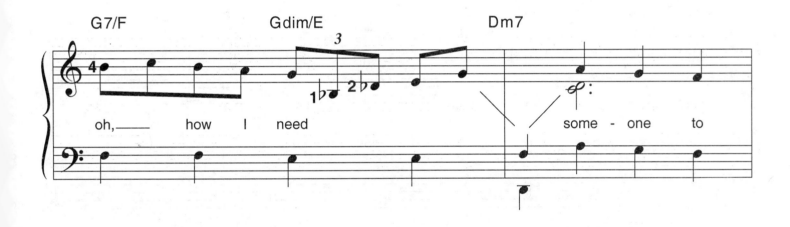

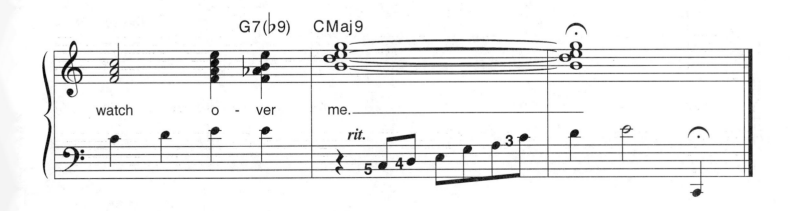

# CHARADE

From the Motion Picture *Charade*

Words by JOHNNY MERCER
Music by HENRY MANCINI
*Arranged by Richard Bradley*

When we played our cha - rade,

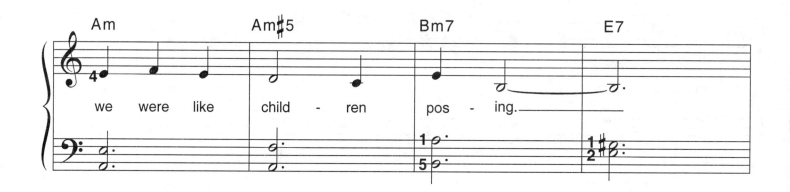

we were like child - ren pos - ing.

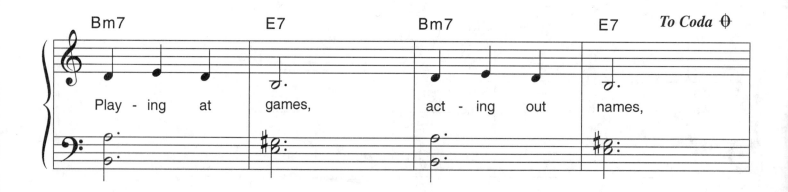

Play - ing at games, act - ing out names,

Charade - 4 - 1

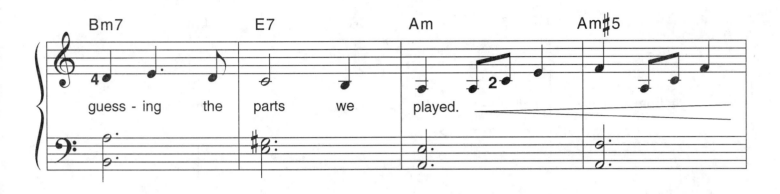

Bm7     E7     Am     Am#5

guess - ing    the    parts    we    played.

Am6     1. Am#5     2. Am#5     Dm7

*mf*                                    Fate

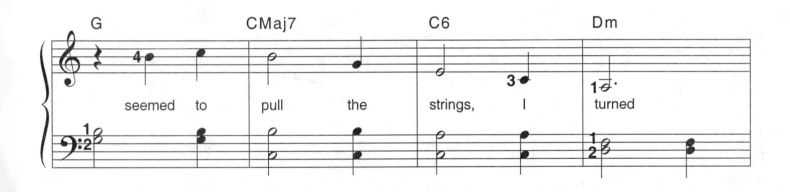

G     CMaj7     C6     Dm

seemed    to    pull    the    strings,    I    turned

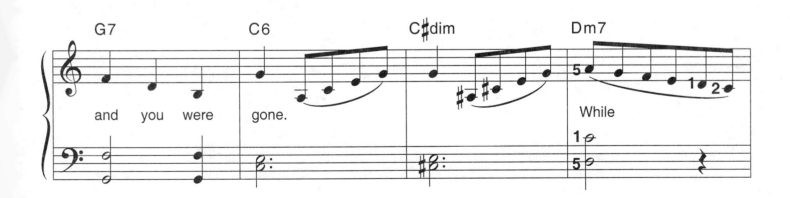

G7     C6     C#dim     Dm7

and    you    were    gone.                             While

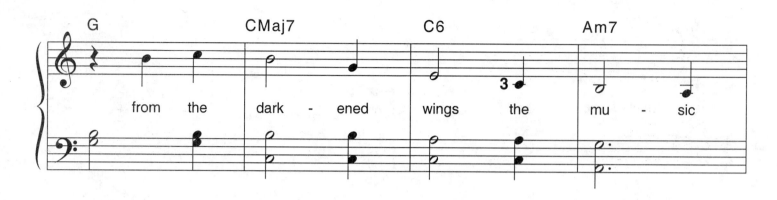

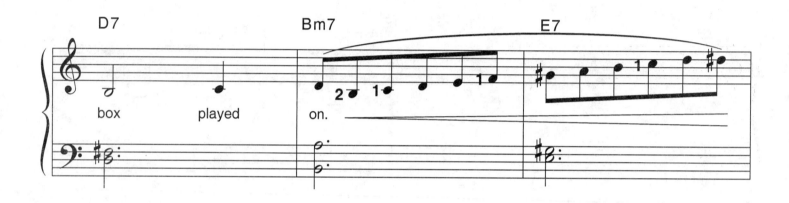

*Coda*

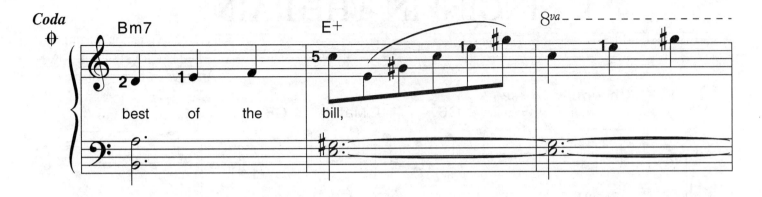

best    of    the    bill,

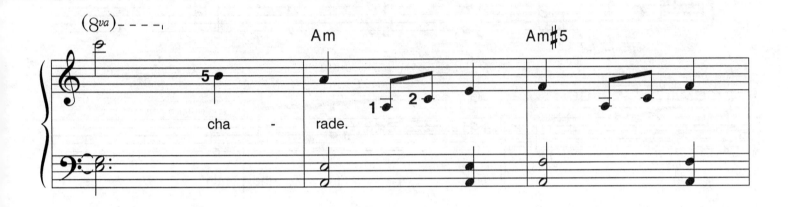

cha - rade.

*rit.*

*Verse 2:*
Oh, what a hit we made.
We came on next to closing.
Best on the bill, lovers until
Love left the masquerade.

*Verse 3:*
Sad little serenade,
Song of my heart's composing.
I hear it still, I always will,
Best of the bill,
Charade.

# SINGIN' IN THE RAIN

From the Motion Picture *Singin' In The Rain*

Lyric by ARTHUR FREED
Music by NACIO HERB BROWN
*Arranged by Richard Bradley*

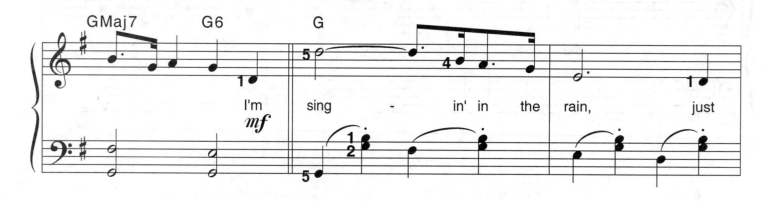

Singin' In The Rain - 3 - 1

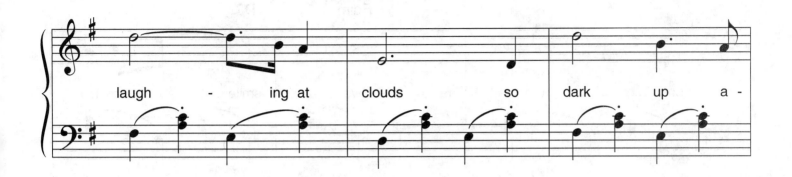

laugh - ing at clouds so dark up a -

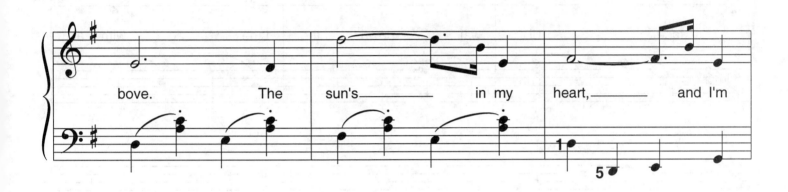

bove. The sun's in my heart, and I'm

read - y for love. Let the storm - y clouds

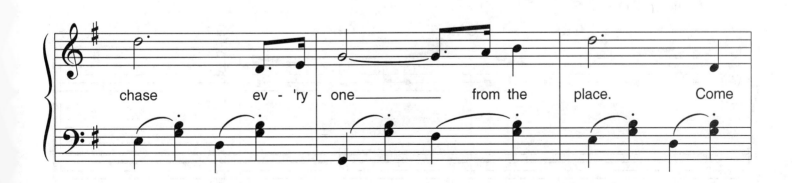

chase ev - 'ry - one from the place. Come

# YOU'RE NEVER FULLY DRESSED
# WITHOUT A SMILE

From the Broadway Musical
*Annie*

Lyrics by MARTIN CHARNIN
Music by CHARLES STROUSE
*Arranged by Richard Bradley*

You're Never Fully Dressed Without A Smile - 3 - 1

# THE GREATEST LOVE OF ALL

From the Motion Picture *The Greatest*

Words by LINDA CREED
Music by MICHAEL MASSER
*Arranged by Richard Bradley*

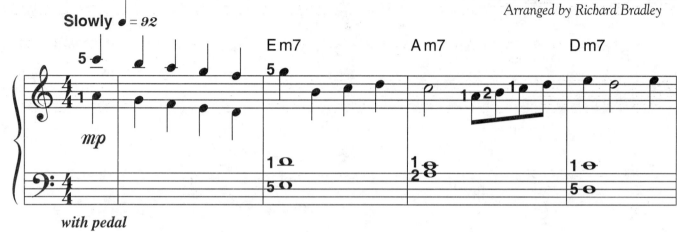

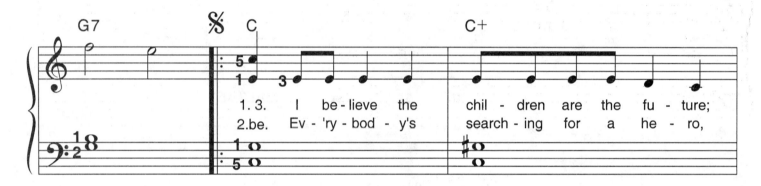

1. 3. I be - lieve the chil - dren are the fu - ture;
2. be. Ev - 'ry - bod - y's search - ing for a he - ro,

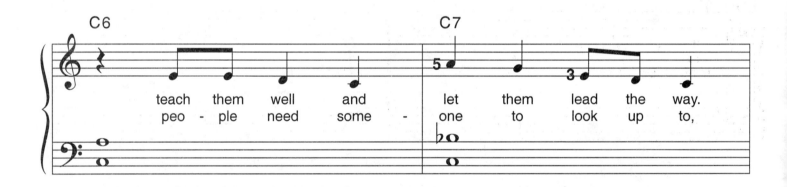

teach them well and let them lead the way.
peo - ple need some - one to look up to,

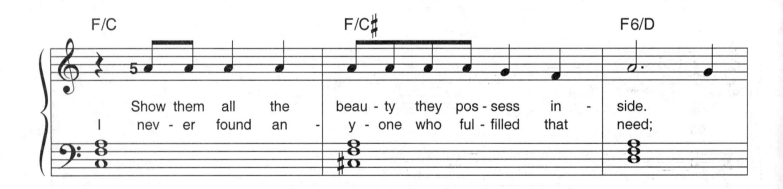

Show them all the beau - ty they pos - sess in - side.
I nev - er found an - y - one who ful - filled that need;

The Greatest Love Of All - 6 - 1

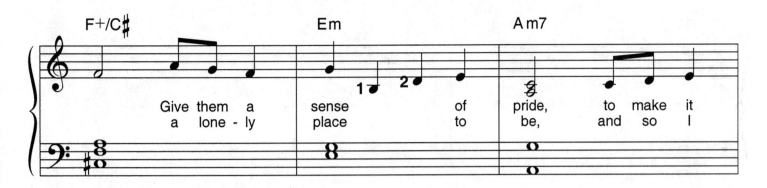

Give them a / a lone - ly | sense / place | of / to | pride, / be, | to make it / and so I

**1.3.**

ea - si - er; | let the chil - dren's | laugh - - - ter | re -

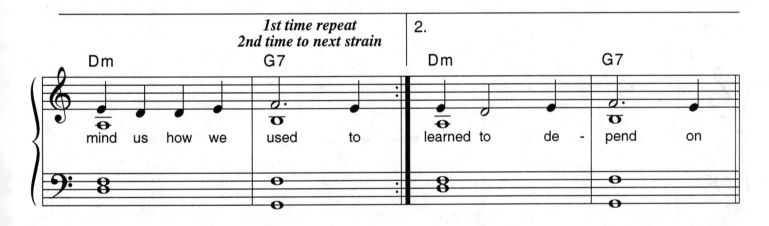

*1st time repeat*
*2nd time to next strain* | **2.**

mind us how we | used to | learned to de - | pend on

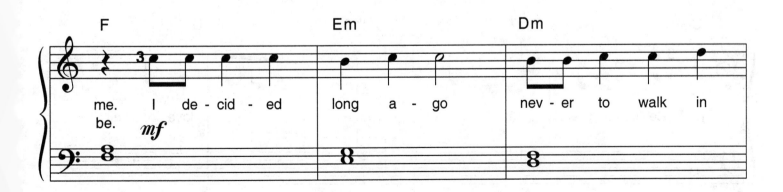

me. I de - cid - ed / be. *mf* | long a - go | nev - er to walk in

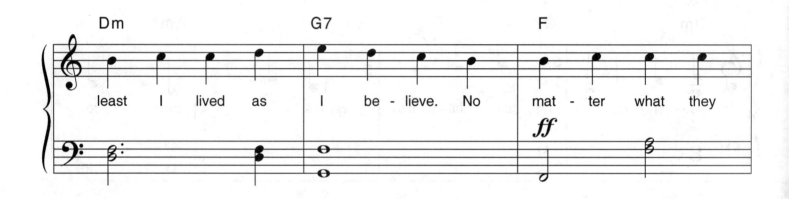

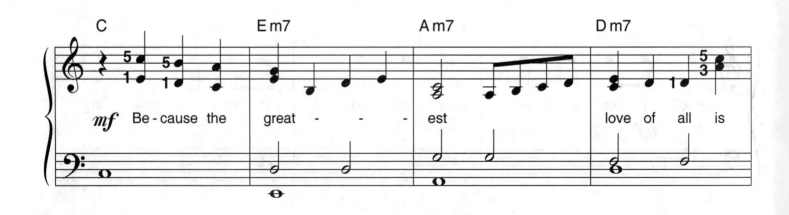

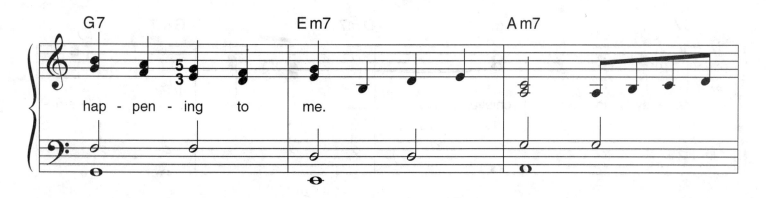

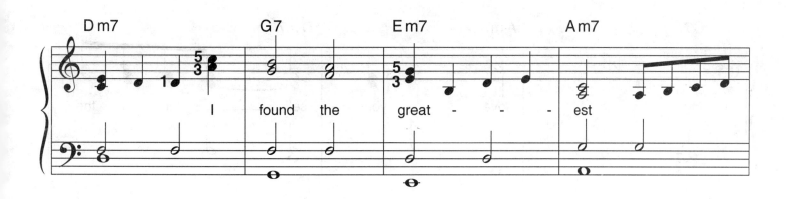

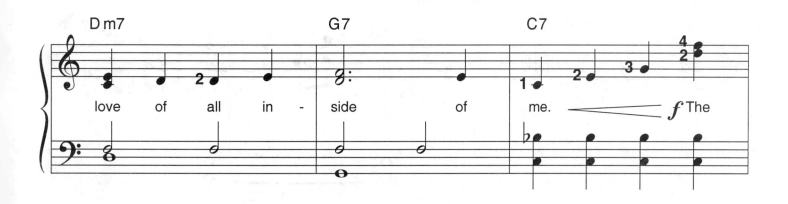

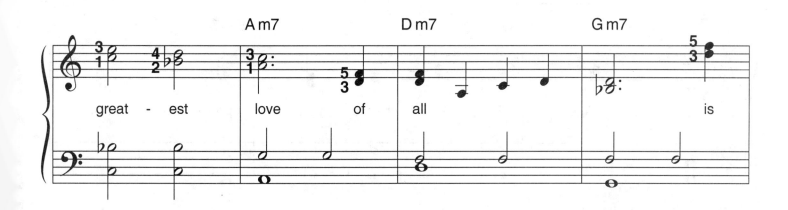

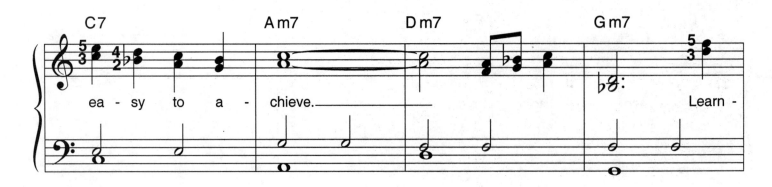

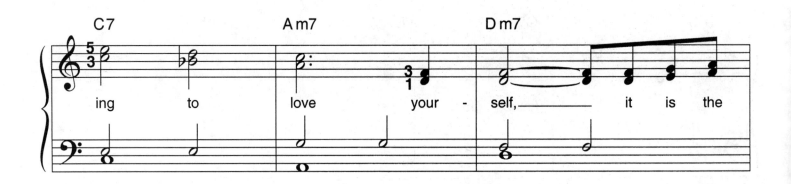

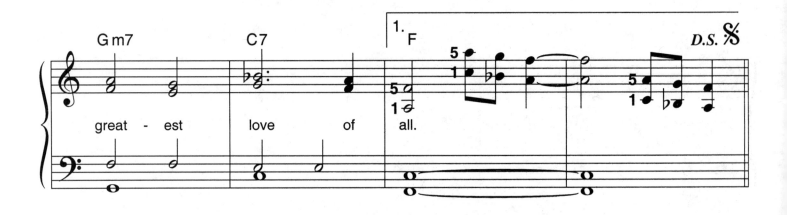

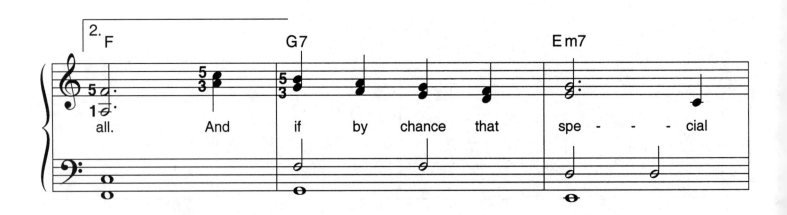

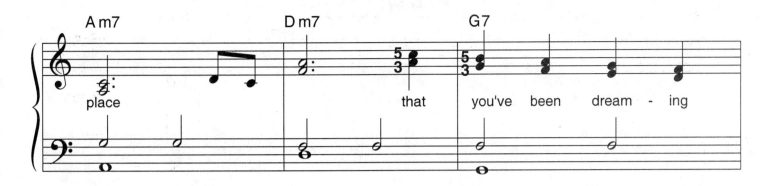

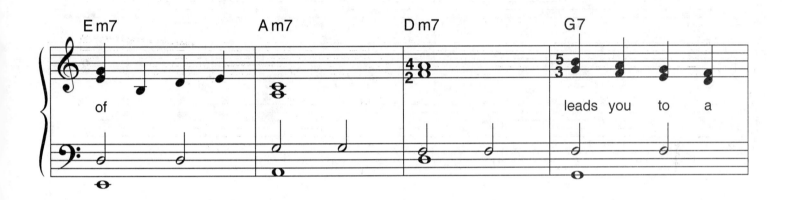

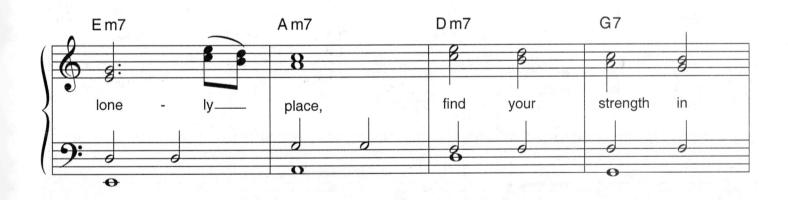

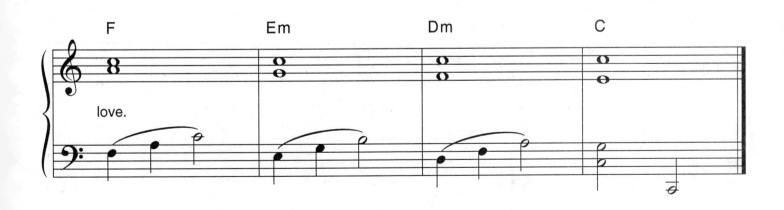

The Greatest Love Of All - 6 - 6

# THE ROSE

From the Motion Picture *The Rose*

Words and Music by
AMANDA MCBROOM
*Arranged by Richard Bradley*

The Rose - 3 - 1

*with pedal*

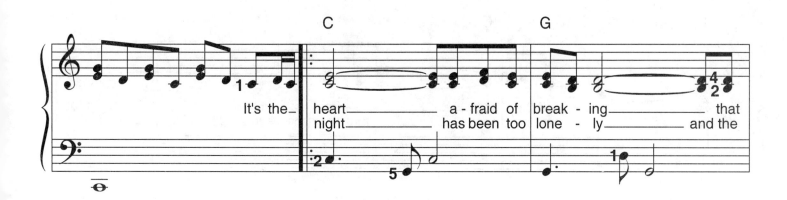

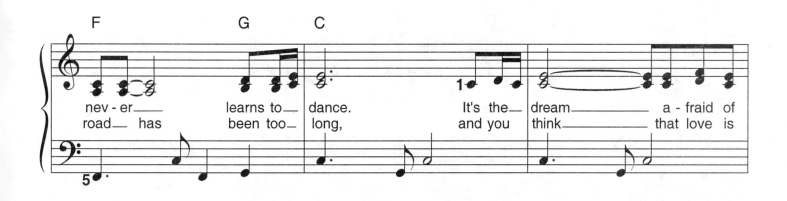

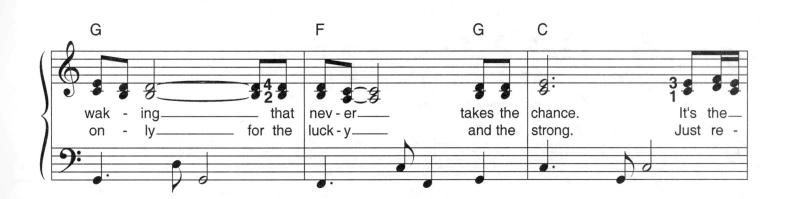

The Rose - 3 - 2

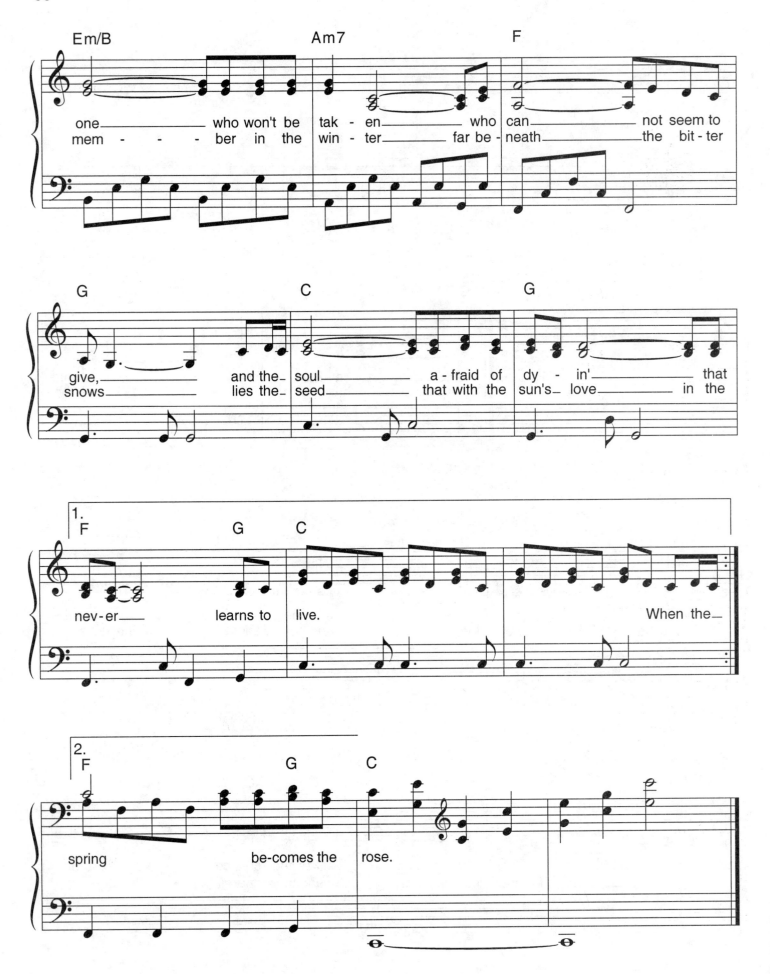

# EBB TIDE

Lyric by
CARL SIGMAN

Music by
ROBERT MAXWELL
*Arranged by Richard Bradley*

Ebb Tide - 3 - 1

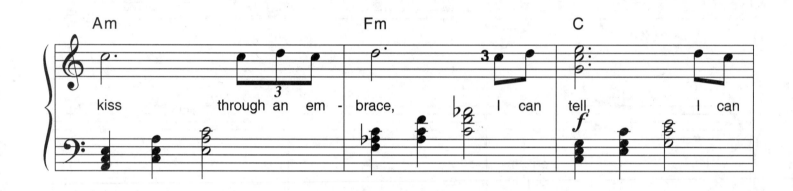

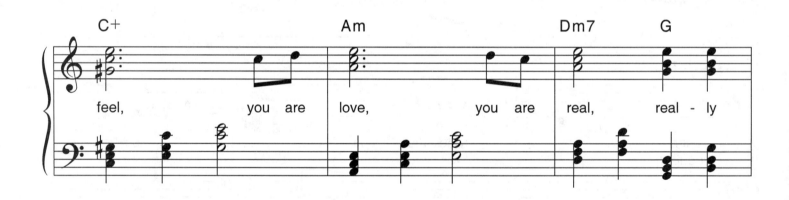

# AIN'T MISBEHAVIN'

Words by
ANDY RAZAF

Music by
THOMAS "FATS" WALLER
and HARRY BROOKS
Arranged by Richard Bradley

Ain't Misbehavin' - 4 - 1

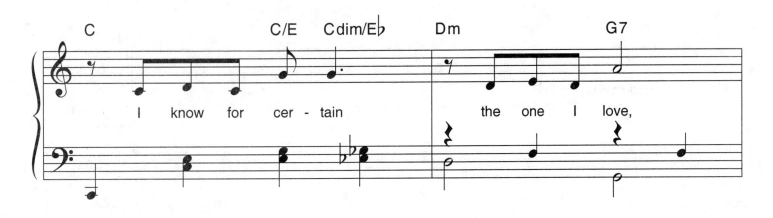

I know for cer - tain the one I love,

I'm thru with flirt - in', it's just you I'm think - ing of,

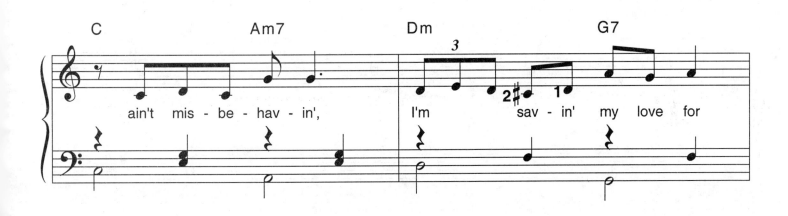

ain't mis - be - hav - in', I'm sav - in' my love for

you.

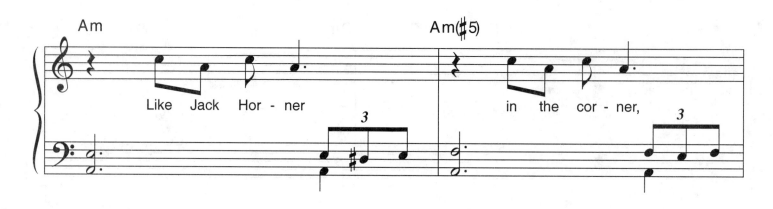

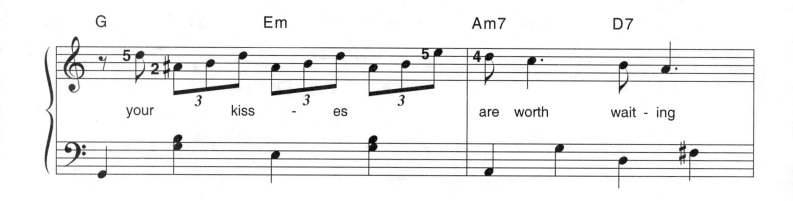

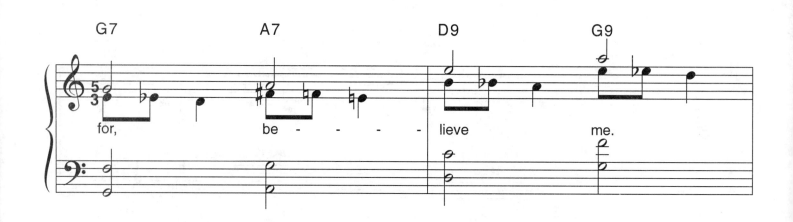

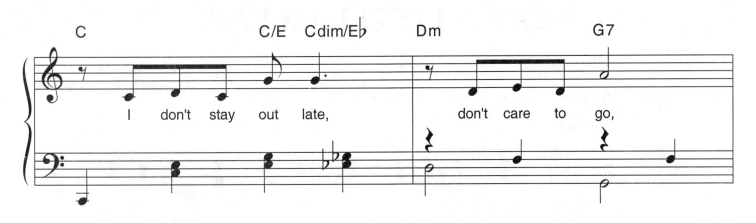

I don't stay out late, don't care to go,

I'm home a-bout eight, just me and my ra-di-o,

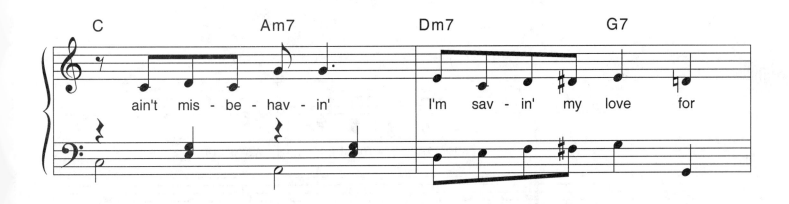

ain't mis-be-hav-in' I'm sav-in' my love for

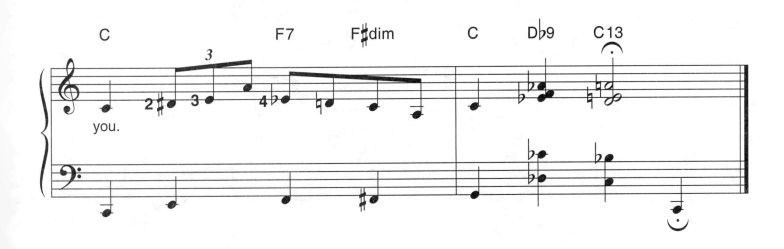

you.

# I SAY A LITTLE PRAYER

Words by
HAL DAVID

Music by
BURT BACHARACH
*Arranged by Richard Bradley*

I Say A Little Prayer - 6 - 2

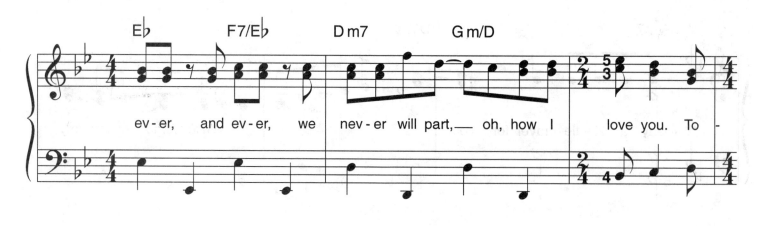

ev-er, and ev-er, we nev-er will part,— oh, how I love you. To-

geth-er, to-geth-er, that's how it should be.— To live with- out you would

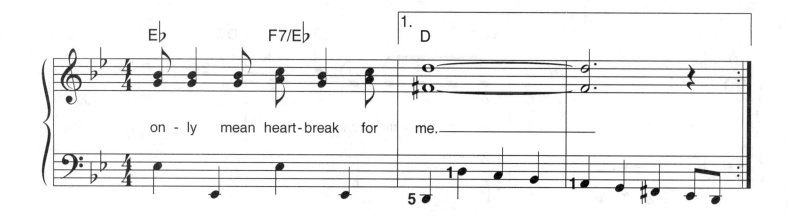

on- ly mean heart-break for me.——

me.——

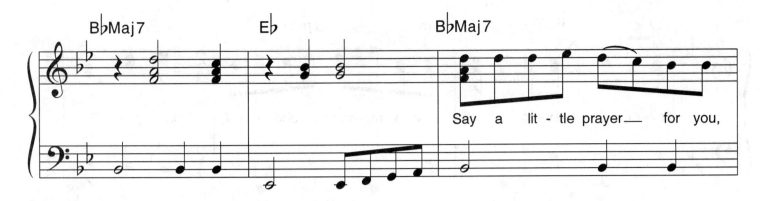

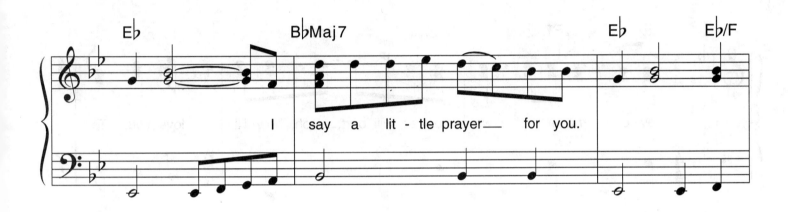

ev - er    and ev - er,    we    nev - er will part,— oh, how I'll    love you. To -

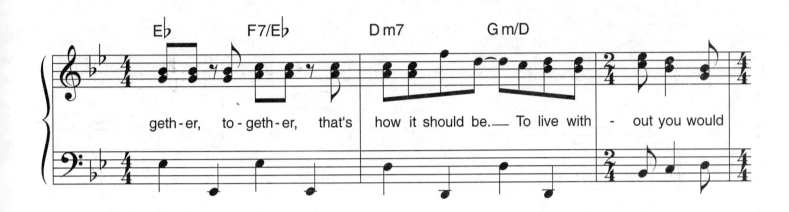

geth - er,    to - geth - er,    that's    how it should be.— To live with    - out you would

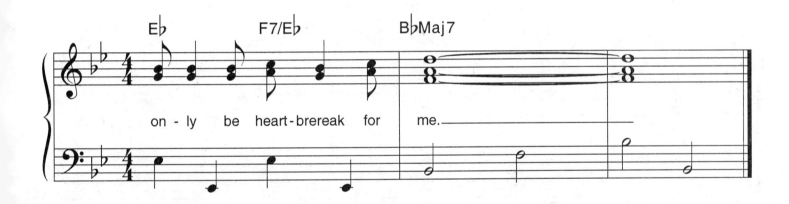

on - ly    be heart - brereak    for    me.—

*Verse 2:*
I run for the bus, dear,
While riding I think of us, dear,
I say a little prayer for you.
At work I just take time
And all through my coffee break time,
I say a little prayer for you.

# THE SUMMER KNOWS

From the Motion Picture *Summer of '42*

Words by MARILYN and ALAN BERGMAN
Music by MICHEL LEGRAND
Arranged by Richard Bradley

The Summer Knows - 3 - 1

which you lie._____ The sum - mer knows,_____ the

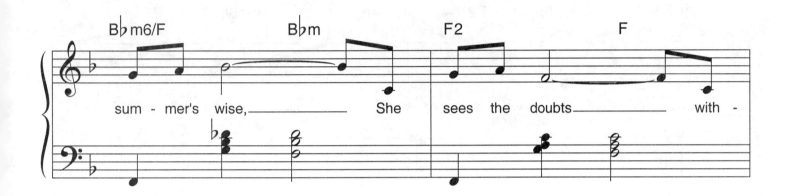

sum - mer's wise,_____ She sees the doubts_____ with -

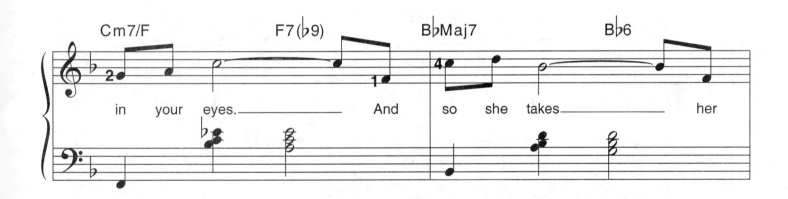

in your eyes._____ And so she takes_____ her

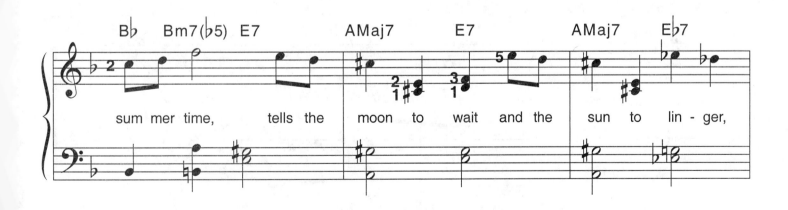

sum mer time, tells the moon to wait and the sun to lin - ger,

54

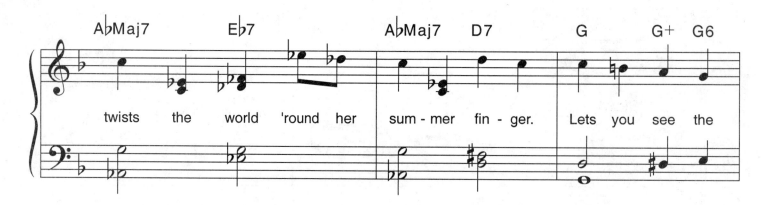

twists the world 'round her sum - mer fin - ger. Lets you see the

won - der of it all. And if you've learned___ your les - son well,___ there's

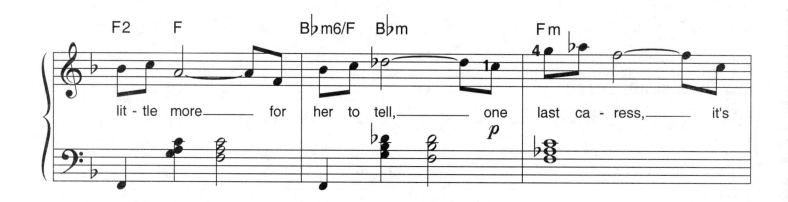

lit - tle more___ for her to tell,___ one last ca - ress,___ it's

time to dress for fall. *molto rit.*

# HOW LONG HAS THIS BEEN GOING ON?

Words by
IRA GERSHWIN

Music by
GEORGE GERSHWIN
*Arranged by Richard Bradley*

How Long Has This Been Going On? - 3 - 1

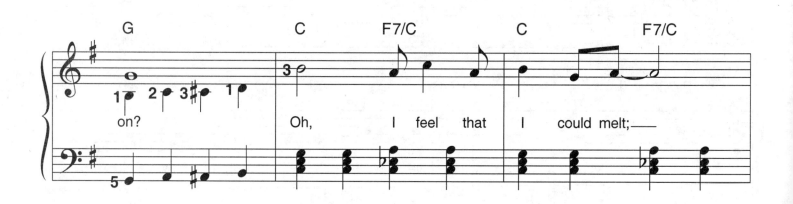

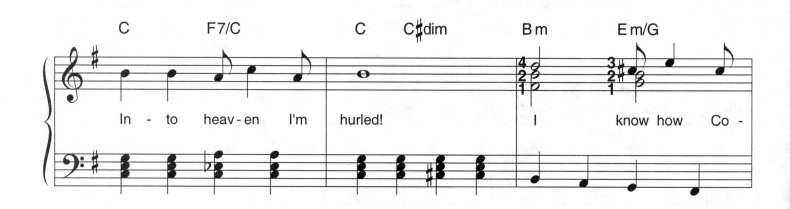

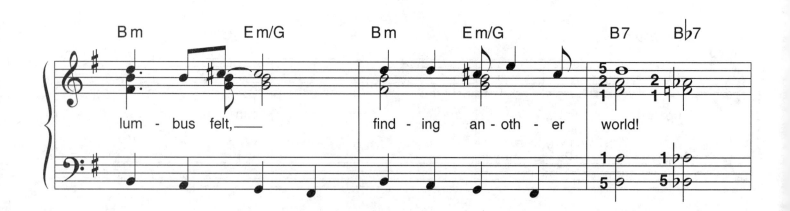

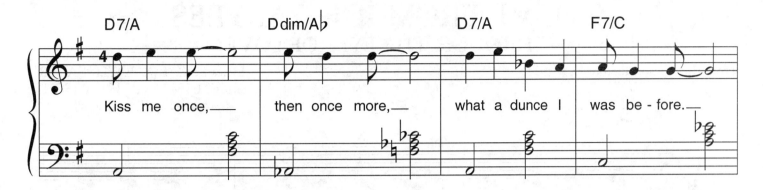

Kiss me once,—— then once more,—— what a dunce I was be-fore.——

What a break!—— For Heav-en's sake!—— How—— long has this been go-ing

on? on?

Verse 2:
I could cry salty tears;
Where have I been all these years?
Listen, you, tell me do,
How long has this been going on?
What a kick! How I buzz!
Boy, you click as no one does!
Hear me sweet, I repeat:
How long has this been going on?
Dear, when in your arms I creep,
That divine rendezvous,
Don't wake me, if I'm asleep,
Let me dream that it's true.
Kiss me twice, then once more,
That makes thrice, let's make it four!
What a break! For Heaven's sake!
How long has this been going on?

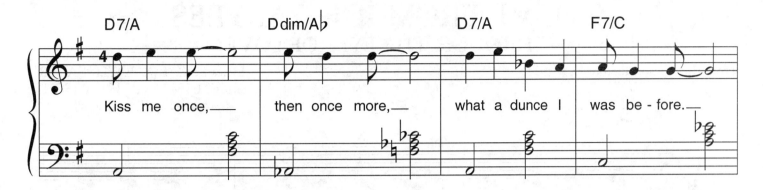

*How Long Has This Been Going On? - 3 - 3*

# THEME FROM ICE CASTLES
## (THROUGH THE EYES OF LOVE)

From the Motion Picture *Ice Castles*

Lyrics by CAROL BAYER SAGER
Music by MARVIN HAMLISCH
*Arranged by Richard Bradley*

Theme From Ice Castles - 4 - 1

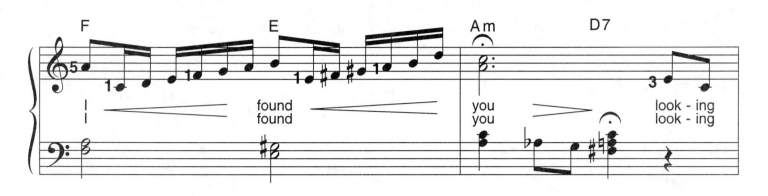

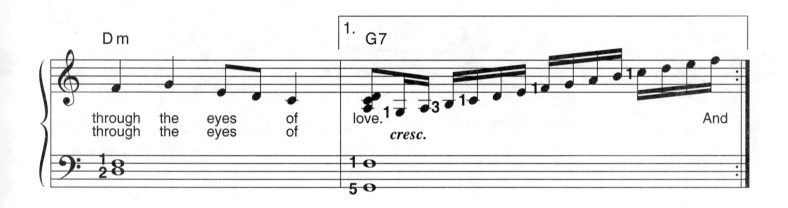

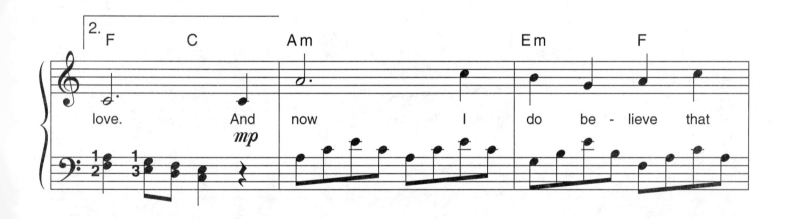

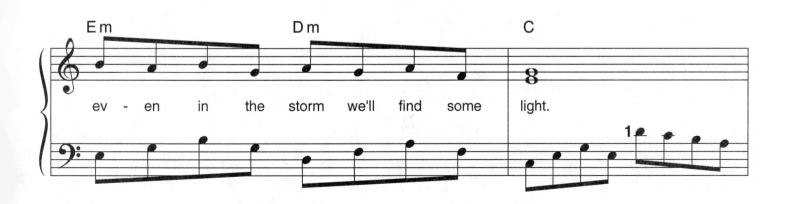

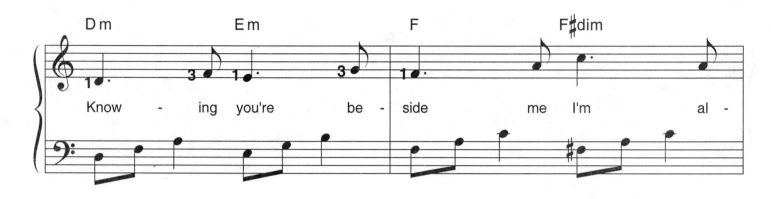

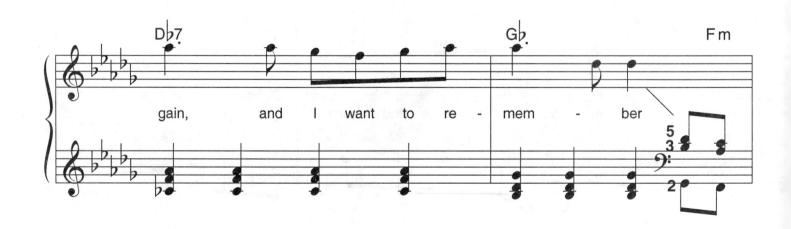

# ALL AT ONCE

Words by
JEFFREY OSBORNE and MICHAEL MASSER

Music by
MICHAEL MASSER
*Arranged by Richard Bradley*

All at once once

fi - n'lly took a
start - ed count - ing

mo - ment and I'm
tear drops and at

re - al - iz - ing
least a mil - lion

All At Once - 4 - 1

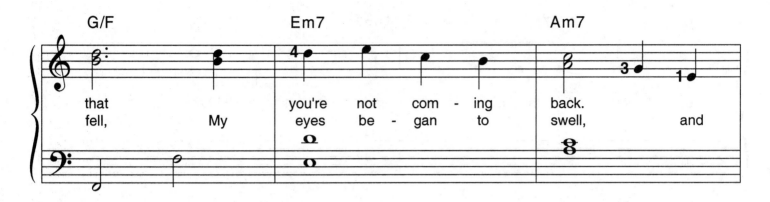

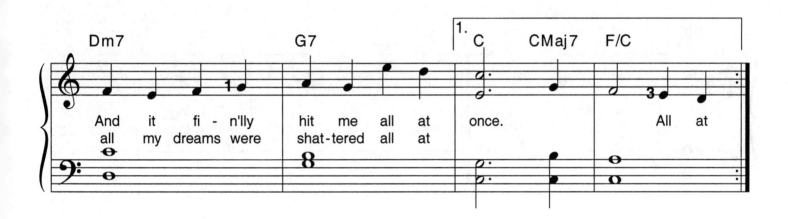

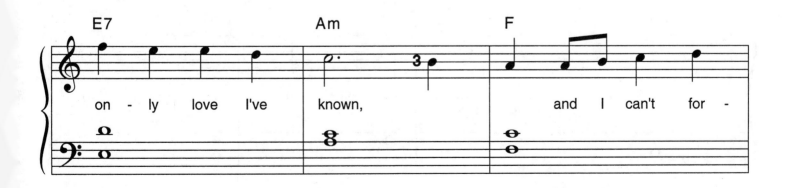

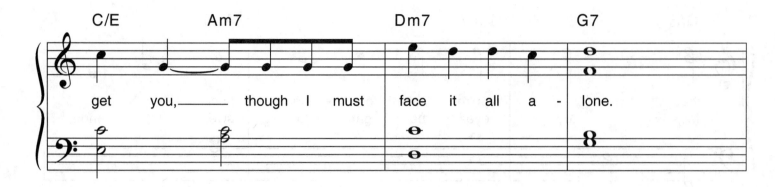

get you,_____ though I must face it all a - lone.

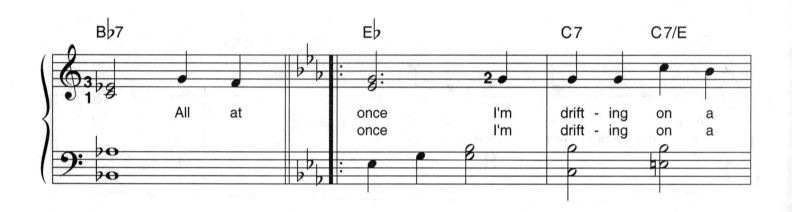

All at once I'm drift - ing on a
once I'm drift - ing on a

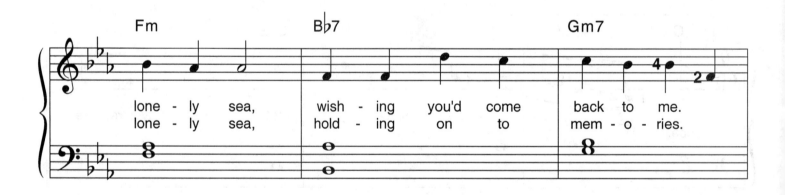

lone - ly sea, wish - ing you'd come back to me.
lone - ly sea, hold - ing on to mem - o - ries.

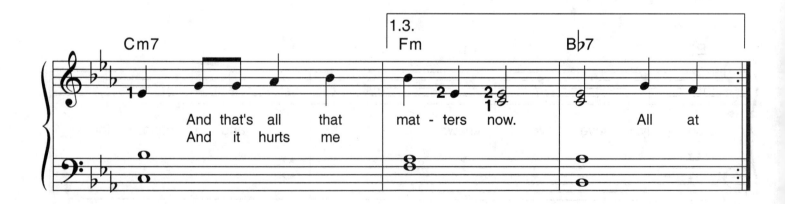

And that's all that mat - ters now. All at
And it hurts me

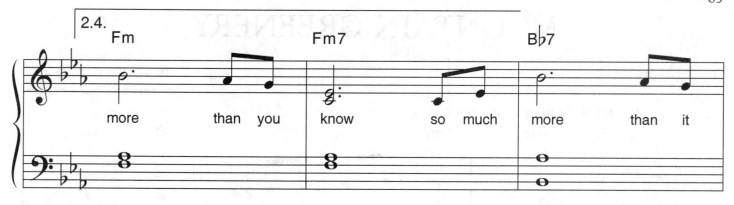

more than you know so much more than it

shows all at once. All at

Verse 2:
All at once
I looked around and found
That you were with another love,
In someone else's arms,
And all my dreams were shattered
All at once.
All at once
The smile that used to greet me
Brightens someone else's day.
She took your smile away,
And left me with just mem'ries
All at once.

# MOUNTAIN GREENERY

Words by
LORENZ HART

Music by
RICHARD RODGERS
*Arranged by Richard Bradley*

Mountain Greenery - 4 - 1

when it rains we'll laugh at the weath - er.

And if your good I'll search for wood,

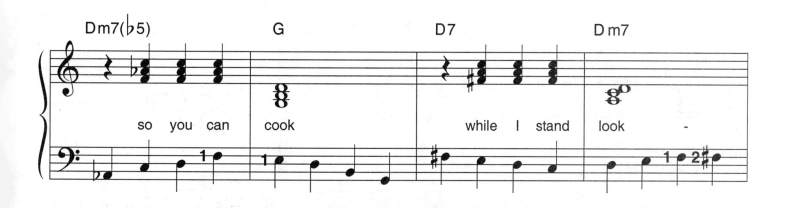

so you can cook while I stand look -

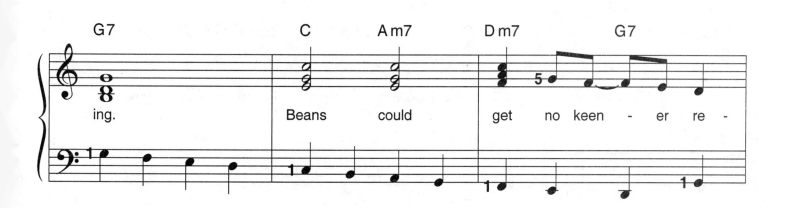

ing. Beans could get no keen - er re -

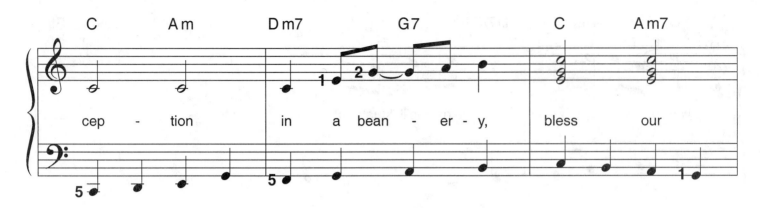

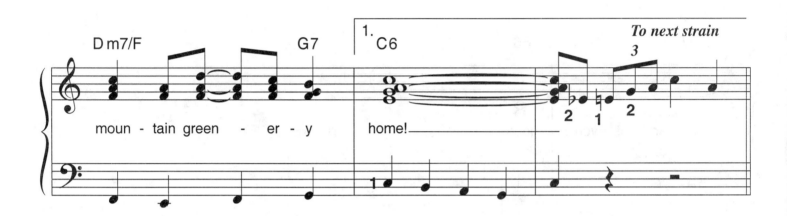

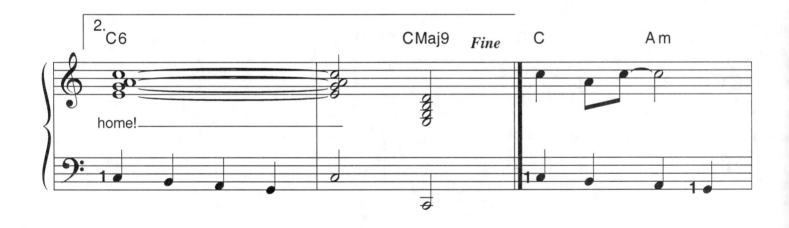

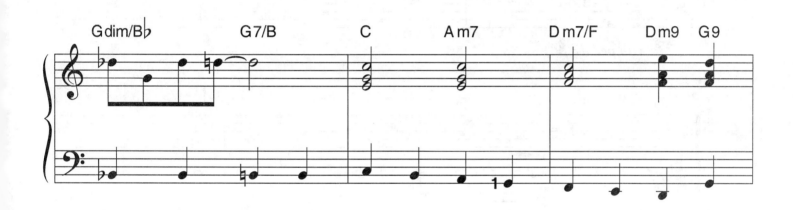

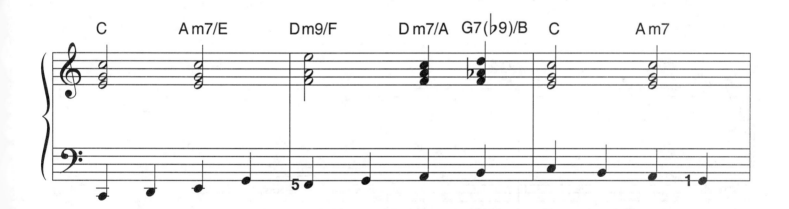

*D.C. al Fine*

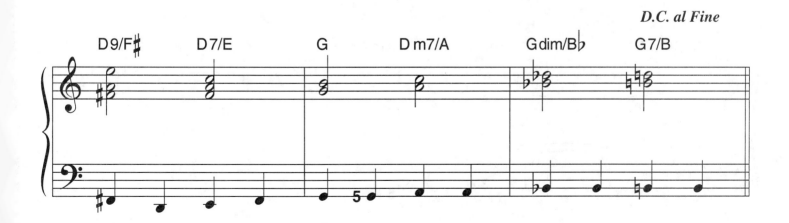

# THE WIND BENEATH MY WINGS

From the Motion Picture *Beaches*

Words and Music by
LARRY HENLEY and JEFF SILBAR
*Arranged by Richard Bradley*

It must have been cold there in my shad - ow,

to nev - er have sun - light on your

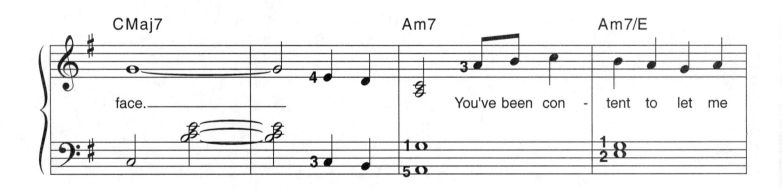

face.___ You've been con - tent to let me

The Wind Beneath My Wings - 4 - 1

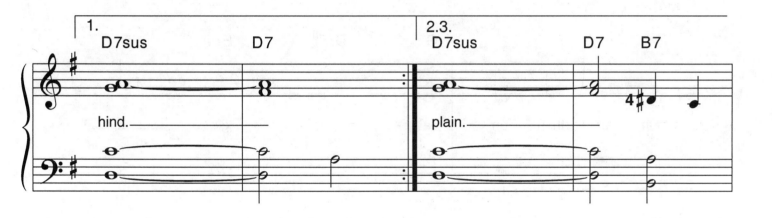

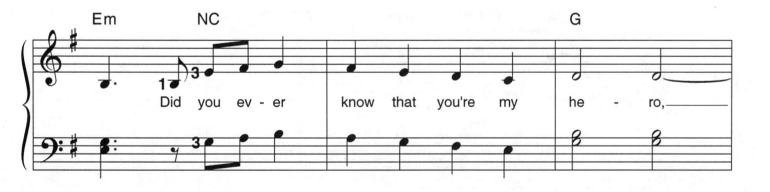

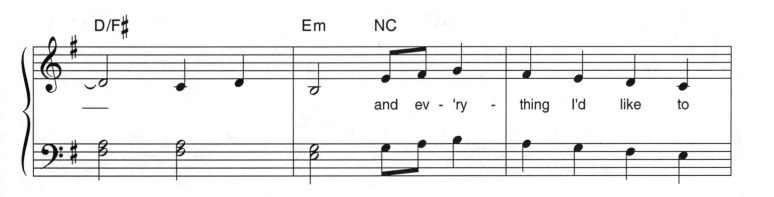

The Wind Beneath My Wings - 4 - 2

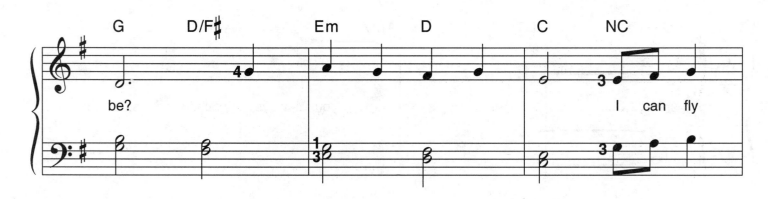

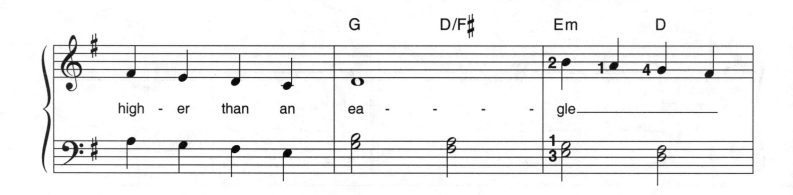

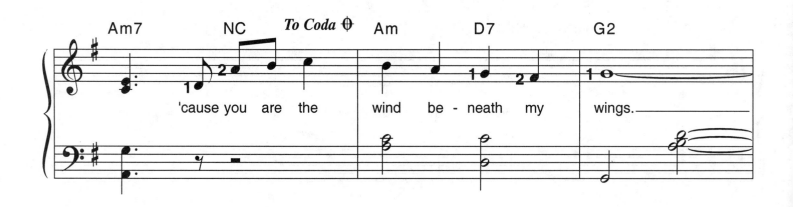

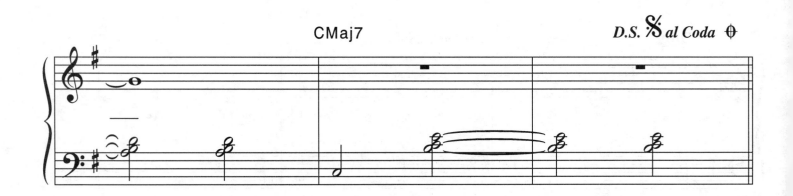

*Coda*

Am — D7 — G2

wind be - neath my wings._____

CMaj7 — G2

You are the wind be - neath my wings.

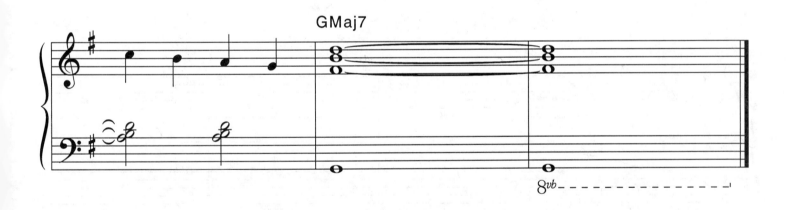

GMaj7

*8vb — — — — — — — — — — — — — —*

*Verse 2:*
I was the one with all the glory
While you were the one with all the strength,
Only a face without a name,
I never once heard you complain.

*Verse 3:*
It might have appeared to go unnoticed
That I've got it all here in my heart.
I want you to know the truth
I would be nothin' without you.

# ON A CLEAR DAY
## (YOU CAN SEE FOREVER)

From the Broadway Musical
*On A Clear Day You Can See Forever*

Lyrics by ALAN JAY LERNER
Music by BURTON LANE
*Arranged by Richard Bradley*

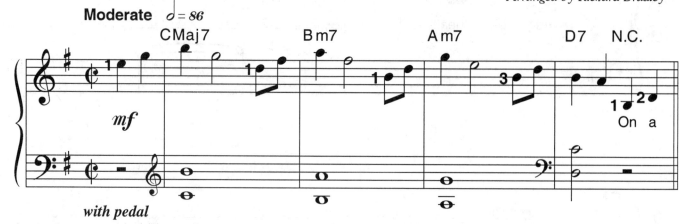

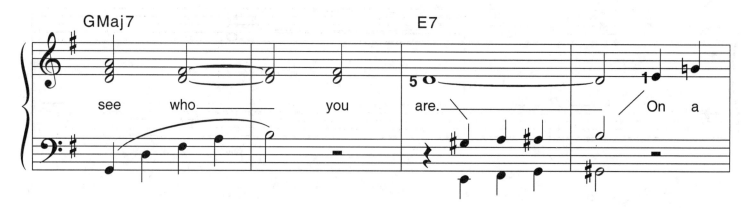

On A Clear Day - 3 - 1

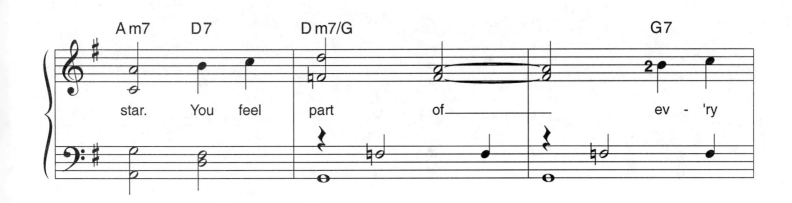

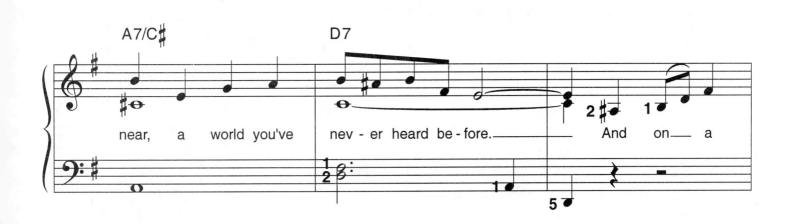

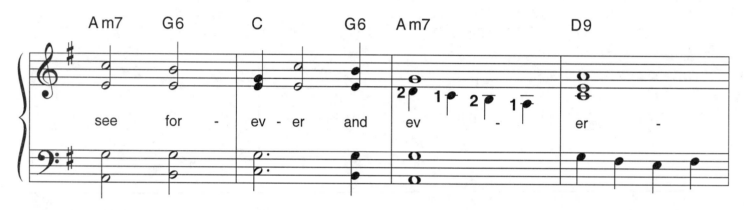

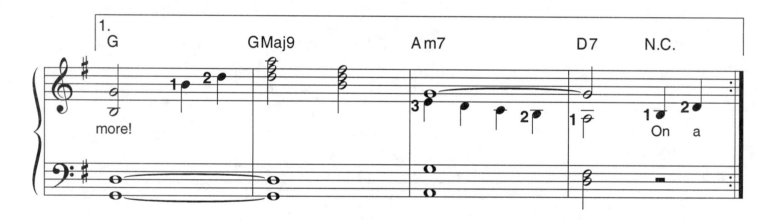

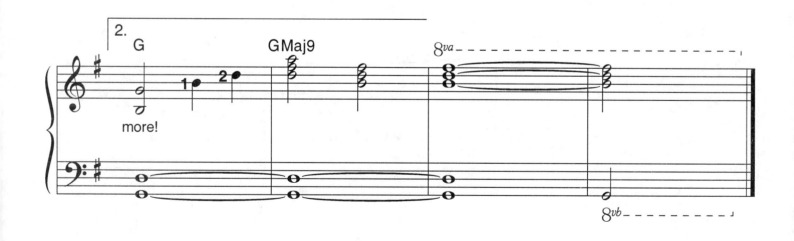

# HE LOVES AND SHE LOVES

From the Broadway Musical *Manhattan*

Music and Lyrics by
GEORGE GERSHWIN
and IRA GERSHWIN
*Arranged by Richard Bradley*

He loves and she loves and they love, so why can't you love and I love, too? Birds love and

*He Loves And She Loves - 3 - 1*

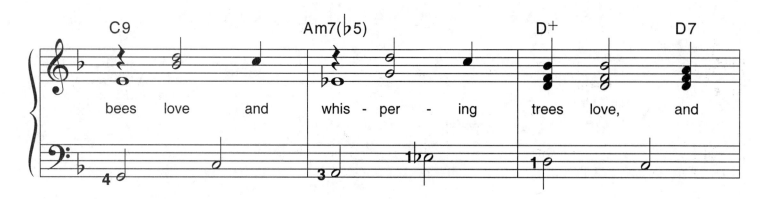

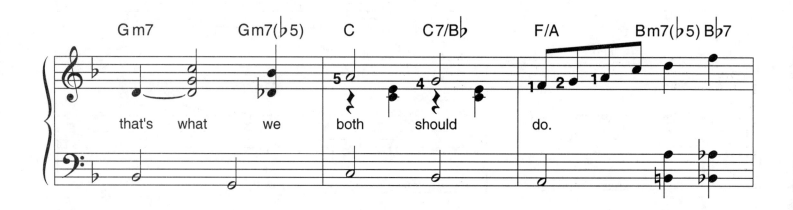

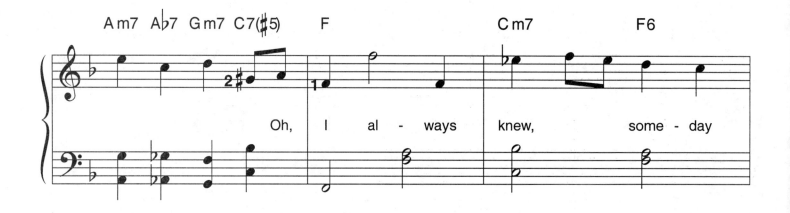

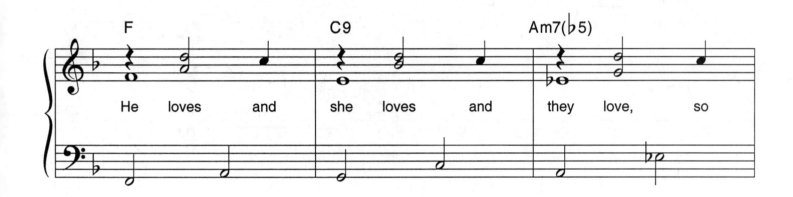

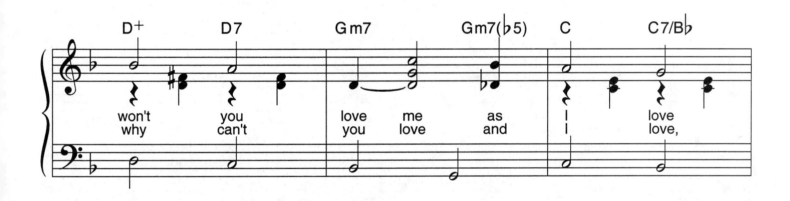

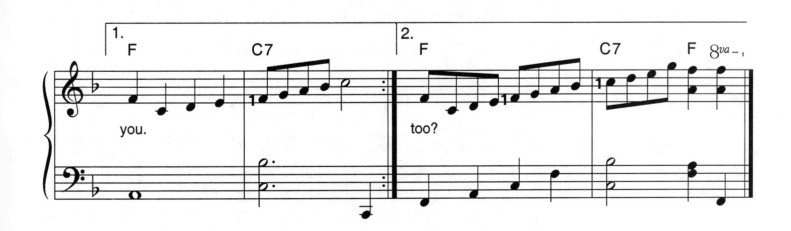

*He Loves And She Loves - 3 - 3*

# (EVERYTHING I DO) I DO IT FOR YOU

From the Motion Picture *Robin Hood: Prince of Thieves*

Written by
BRYAN ADAMS, ROBERT JOHN LANGE
and MICHAEL KAMEN
*Arranged by Richard Bradley*

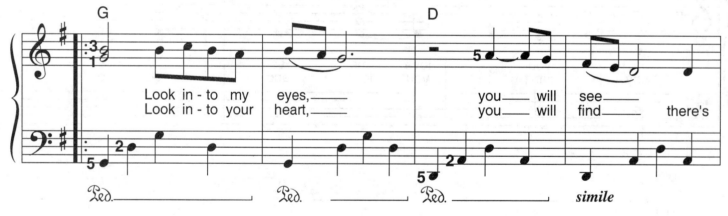

Look in-to my eyes,——— you— will see———
Look in-to your heart,——— you— will find——— there's

what you mean to me.———
noth - ing there to hide.———

Search——— your
So take me

(Everything I Do) I Do It For You - 5 - 1

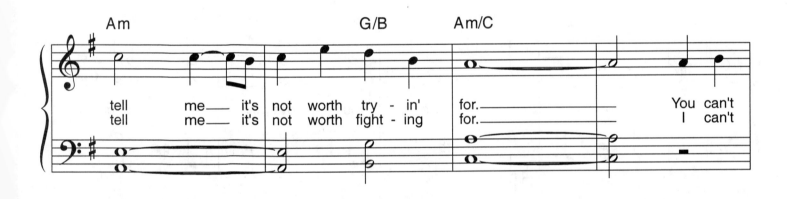

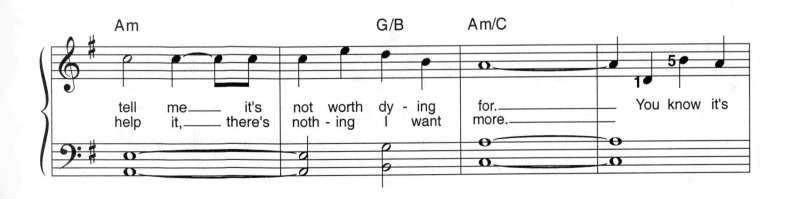

(Everything I Do) I Do It For You - 5 - 2

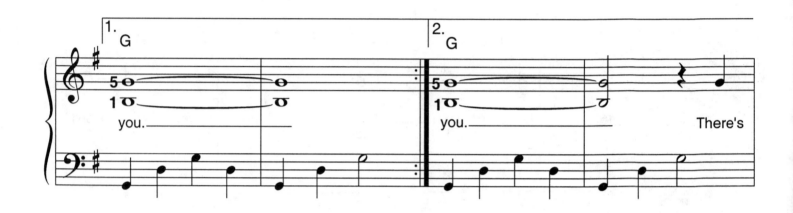

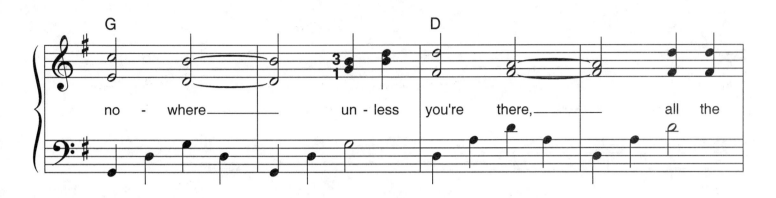

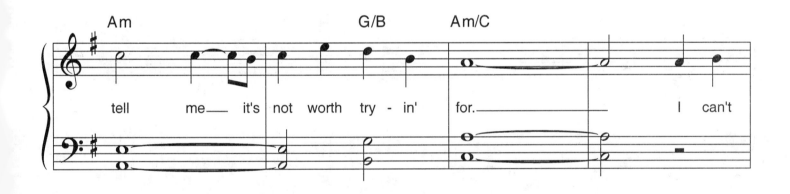

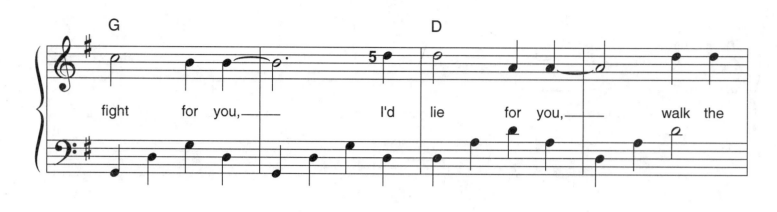

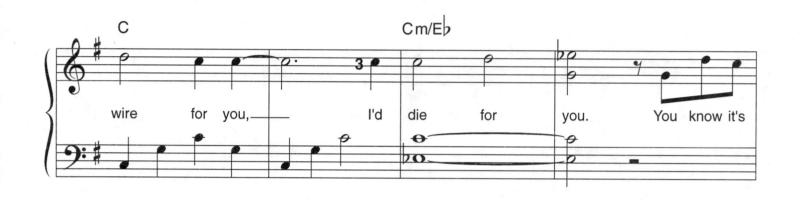

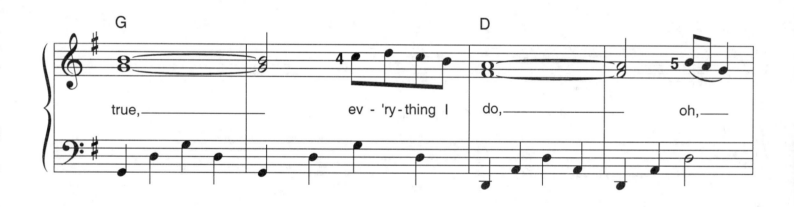

# WHERE OR WHEN

From the Broadway Musical *Babes In Arms*

Words by LORENZ HART
Music by RICHARD RODGERS
*Arranged by Richard Bradley*

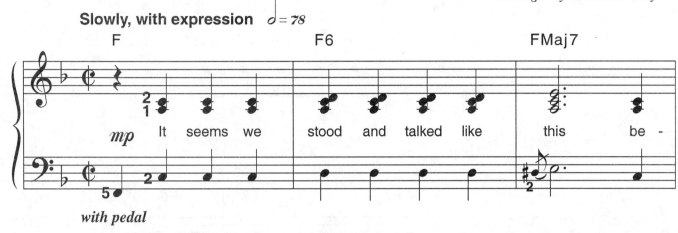

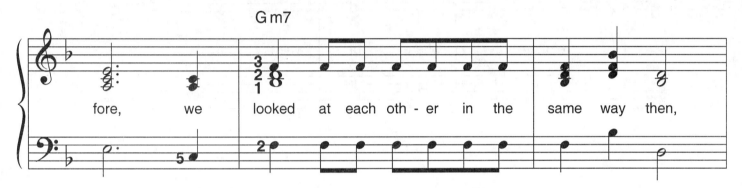

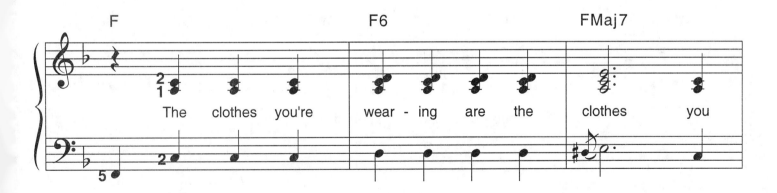

Where Or When - 3 - 1

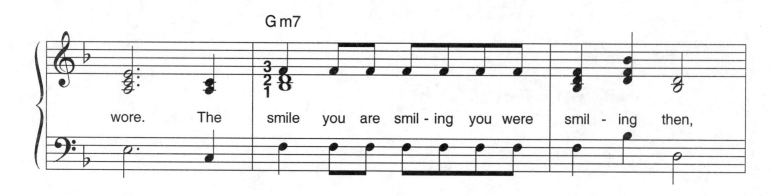

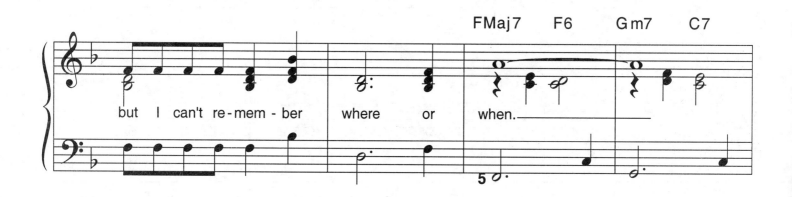

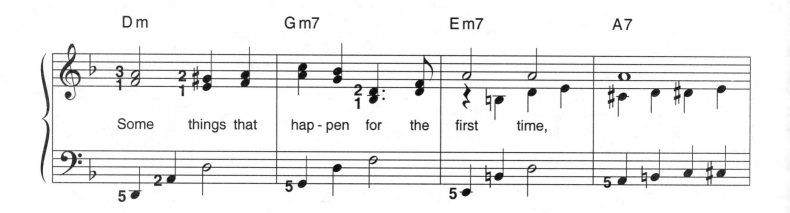

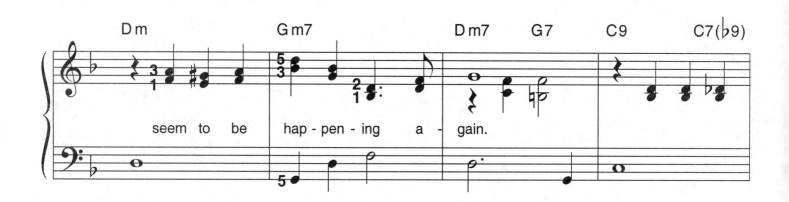

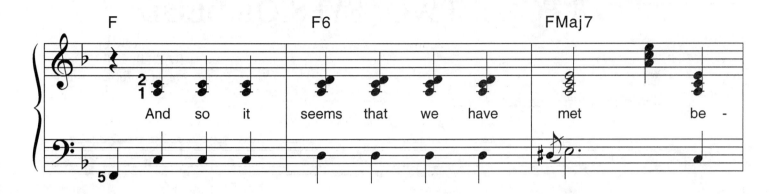

F           F6           FMaj7

And so it seems that we have met be -

F+           Gm           Am

fore, and laughed be - fore, and

*cresc*

Gm           Am           Gm

loved be - fore, but who knows

*f*          *rit.*

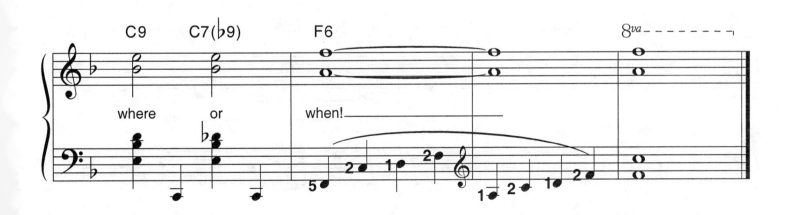

C9    C7(♭9)          F6          *8va - - - - - - -*

where or when!_____

# FIVE FOOT TWO, EYES OF BLUE

Words by
JOE YOUNG
and SAM LEWIS

Music by
RAY HENDERSON
*Arranged by Richard Bradley*

Five Foot Two, Eyes Of Blue - 4 - 1

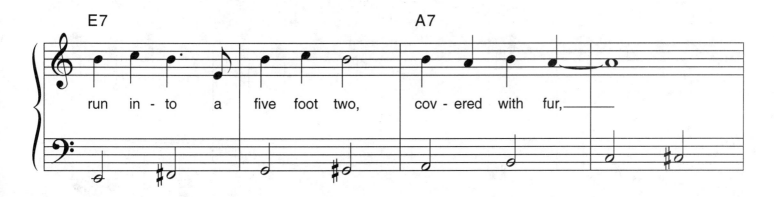

run in - to a five foot two, cov - ered with fur,

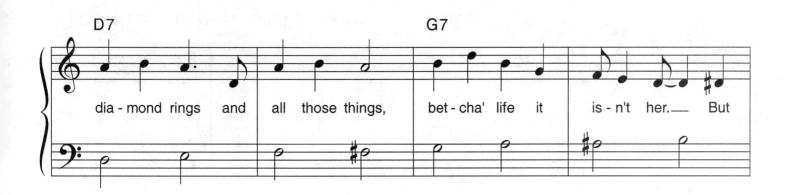

dia - mond rings and all those things, bet - cha' life it is - n't her.— But

could she love, could she woo? Could she, could she, could she coo?— Has

an - y - bod - y seen my girl?

Five Foot Two, Eyes Of Blue - 4 - 2

Five Foot Two, Eyes Of Blue - 4 - 4

# CAN'T TAKE MY EYES OFF OF YOU

Words and Music by
**BOB CREWE and BOB GAUDIO**
*Arranged by Richard Bradley*

*Can't Take My Eyes Off Of You - 4 - 1*

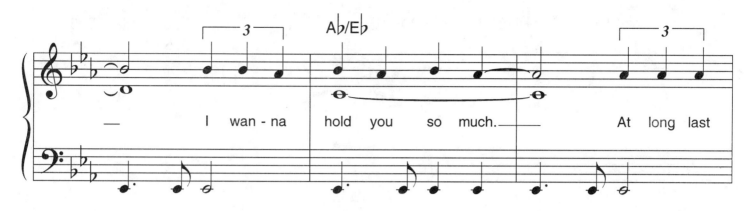

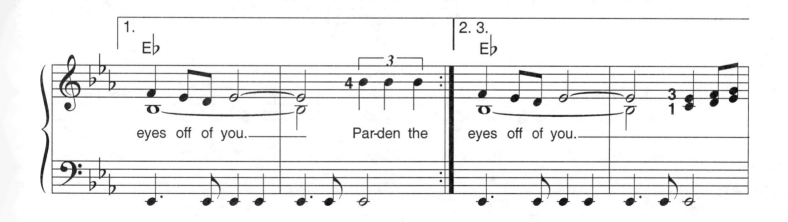

Can't Take My Eyes Off Of You - 4 - 2

94

Verse 2:
Pardon the way that I stare,
There's nothing else to compare,
The sight of you leaves me weak,
There are no words left to speak.
But if you feel like I feel,
Please let me know that it's real.

# JUST YOU, JUST ME

Lyric by
RAYMOND KLAGES

Music by
JESSE GREER
*Arranged by Richard Bradley*

Just You, Just Me - 2 - 1

# MY FUNNY VALENTINE

From the Broadway Musical *Babes In Arms*
and the Motion Picture *Pal Joey*

Words by LORENZ HART
Music by RICHARD RODGERS
*Arranged by Richard Bradley*

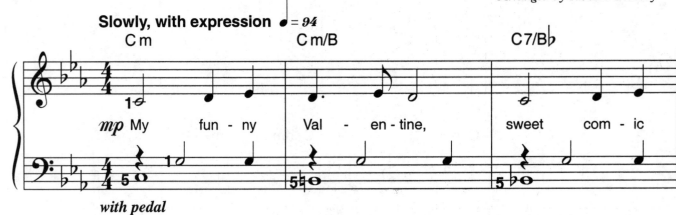

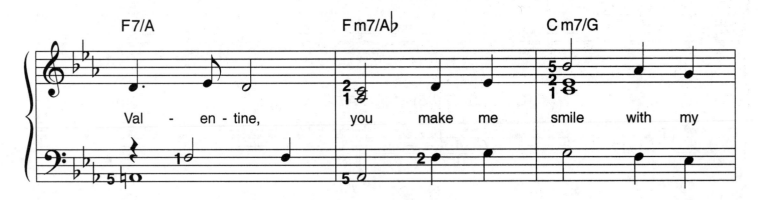

My Funny Valentine - 3 - 1

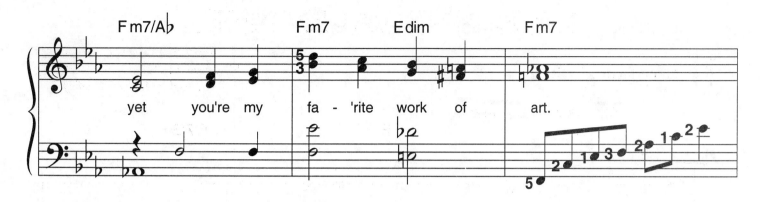

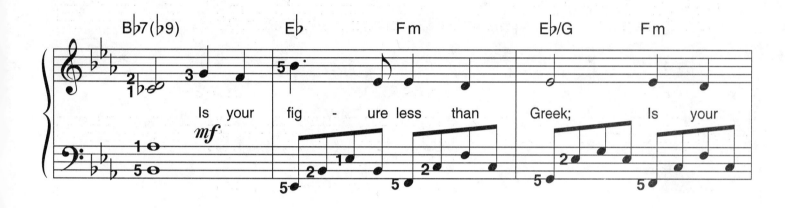

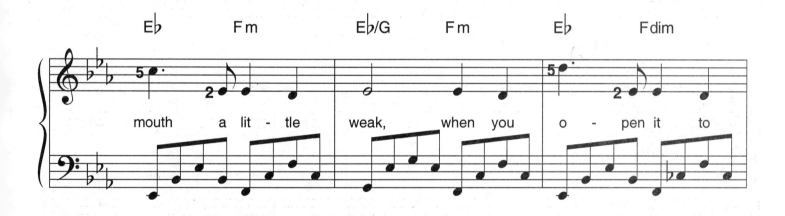

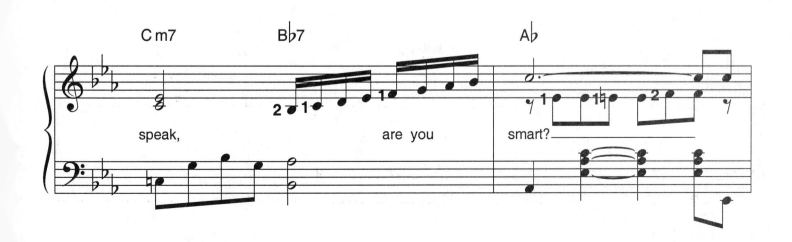

My Funny Valentine - 3 - 2

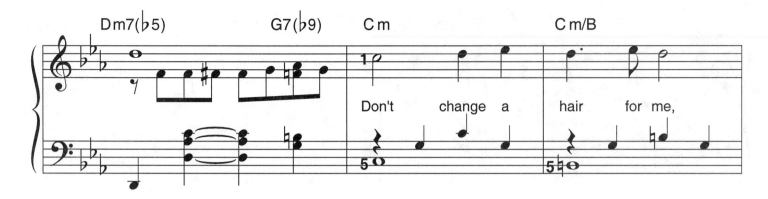

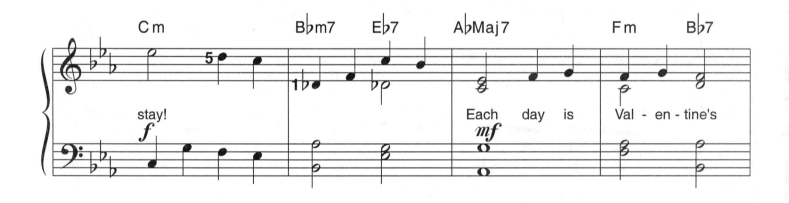

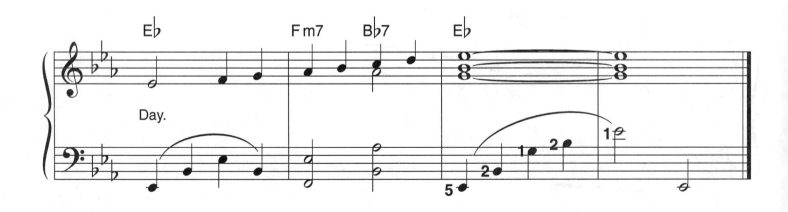

My Funny Valentine - 3 - 3

# BLUE MOON

Lyrics by
LORENZ HART

Music by
RICHARD RODGERS
*Arranged by Richard Bradley*

Blue Moon - 3 - 1

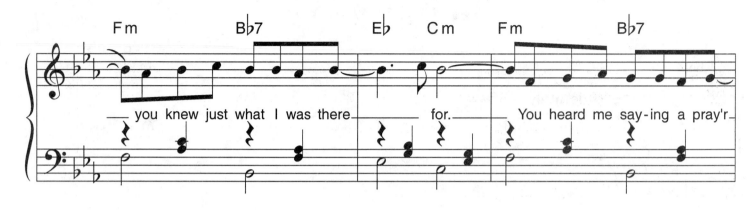

you knew just what I was there ___ for. ___ You heard me say-ing a pray'r ___

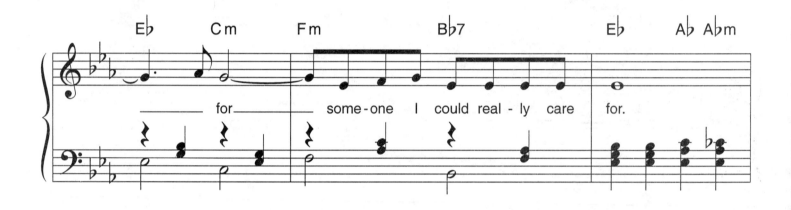

___ for ___ some-one I could real - ly care for.

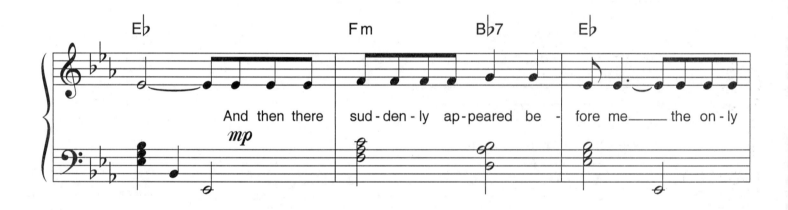

And then there sud-den-ly ap-peared be - fore me ___ the on-ly

*mp*

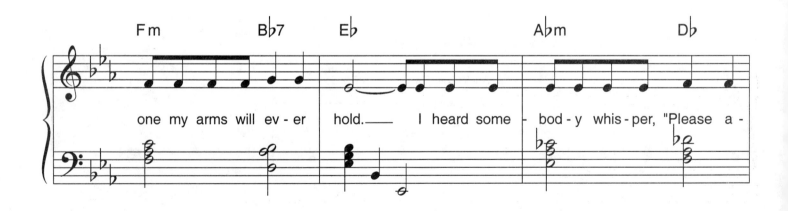

one my arms will ev - er hold. ___ I heard some - bod - y whis-per, "Please a -

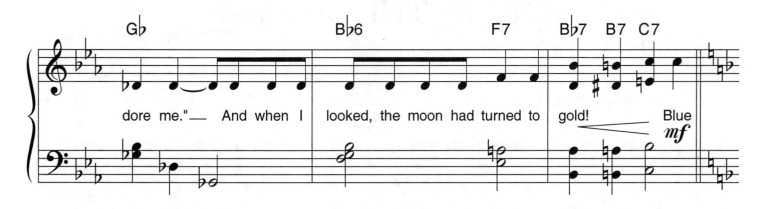

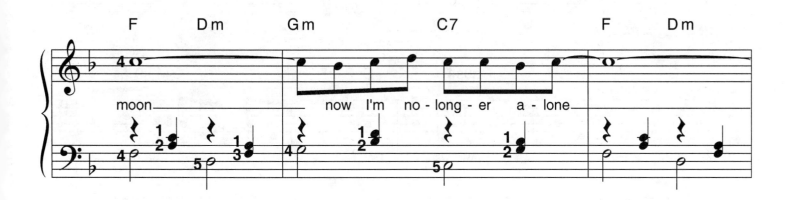

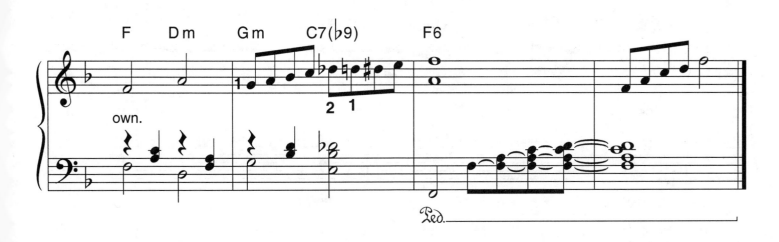

# SEND IN THE CLOWNS

From the Broadway Musical *A Little Night Music*

Words and Music by
STEPHEN SONDHEIM
*Arranged by Richard Bradley*

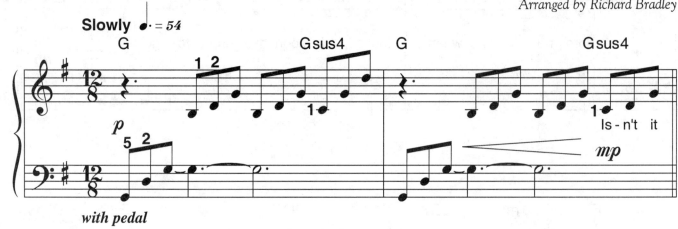

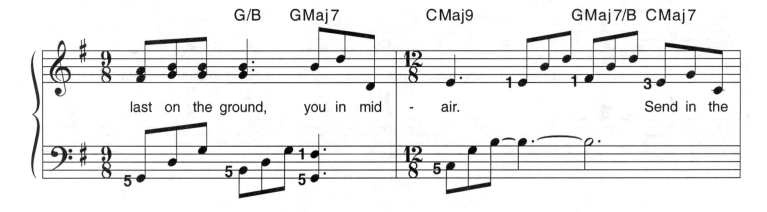

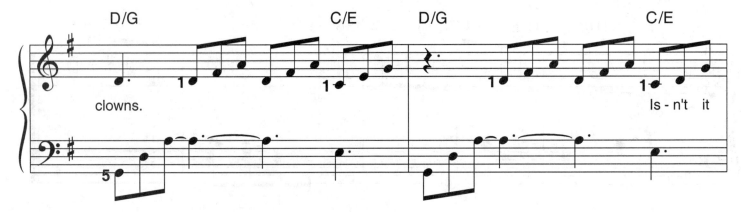

Send In The Clowns - 4 - 1

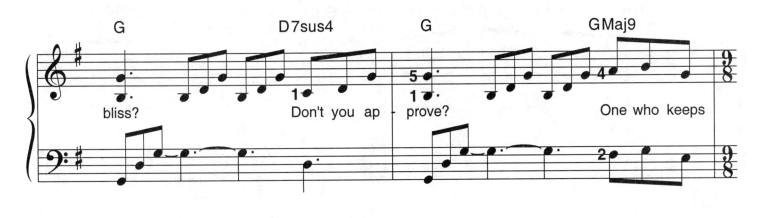

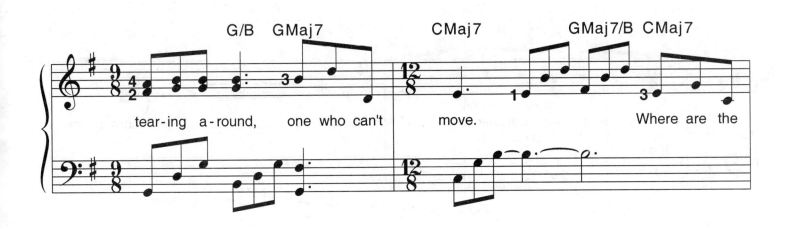

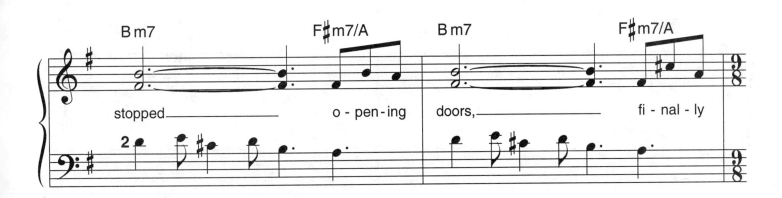

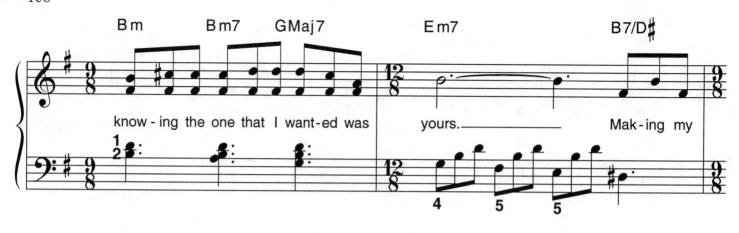

know - ing the one that I want-ed was yours._____ Mak-ing my

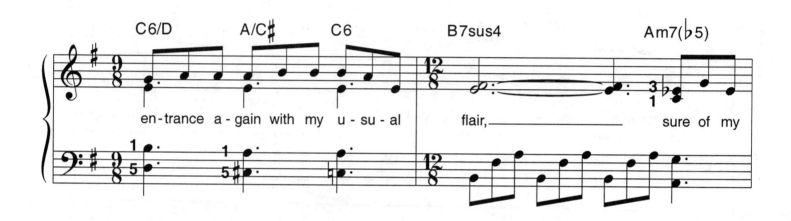

en - trance a - gain with my u - su - al flair,_____ sure of my

lines,_____ no one is there.

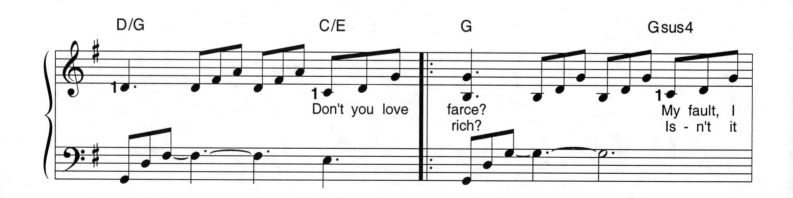

Don't you love farce?

rich?

My fault, I

Is - n't it

# YOU LIGHT UP MY LIFE

Words and Music by
JOE BROOKS
*Arranged by Richard Bradley*

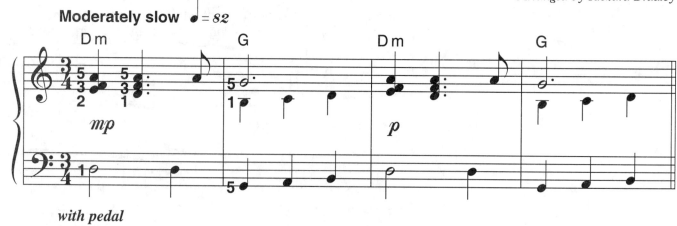

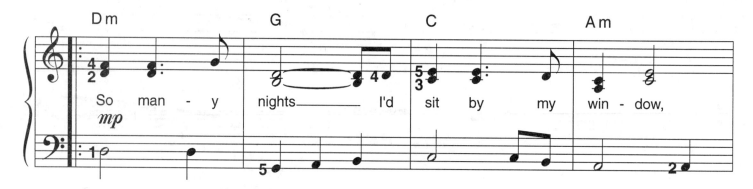

So man - y nights_____ I'd sit by my win - dow,

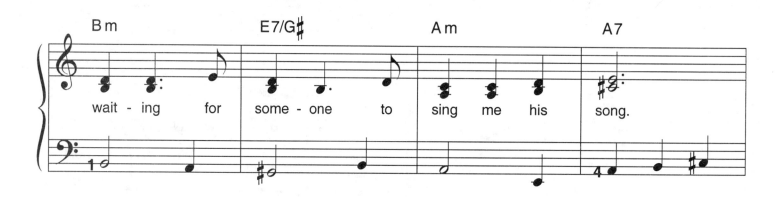

wait - ing for some - one to sing me his song.

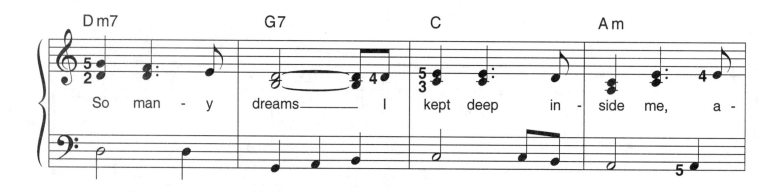

So man - y dreams_____ I kept deep in - side me, a-

You Light Up My Life - 4 - 1

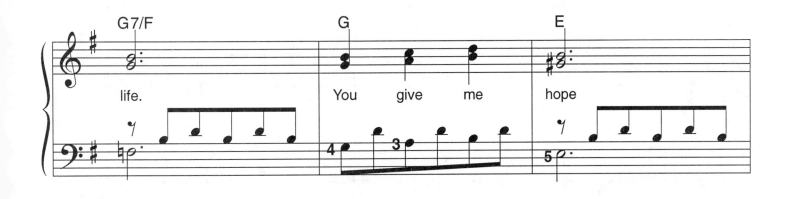

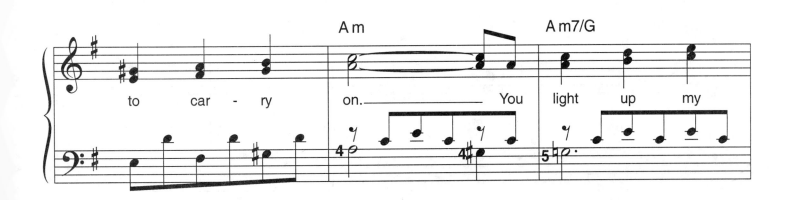

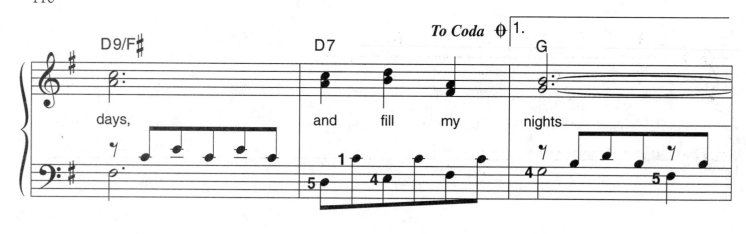

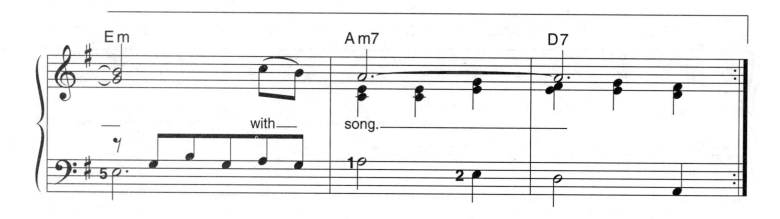

*Verse 2*:
Rollin' at sea, adrift on the waters,
Could it be finally I'm turning for home?
Finally a chance to say, "Hey! I love you."
Never again to be all alone.
*Chorus*:

# DEAR HEART

From the Motion Picture *Dear Heart*

Words by JAY LIVINGSTON and RAY EVANS
Music by HENRY MANCINI
*Arranged by Richard Bradley*

sin - gle room, a ta - ble for one; it's a

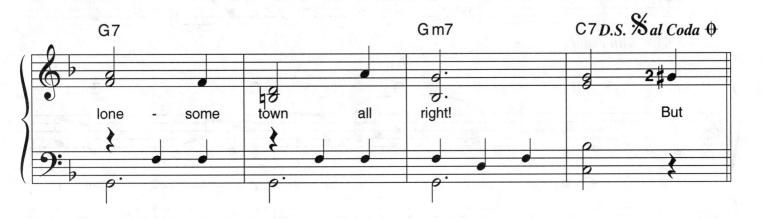

lone - some town all right! But

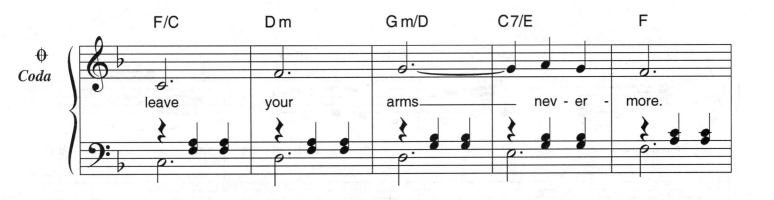

leave your arms_____ nev - er - more.

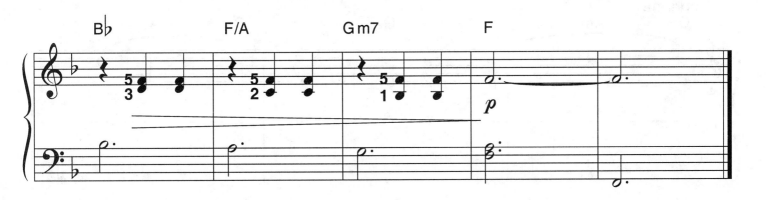

# I WILL ALWAYS LOVE YOU

From the Motion Picture Soundtrack *The Bodyguard*

Words and Music by
DOLLY PARTON
*Arranged by Richard Bradley*

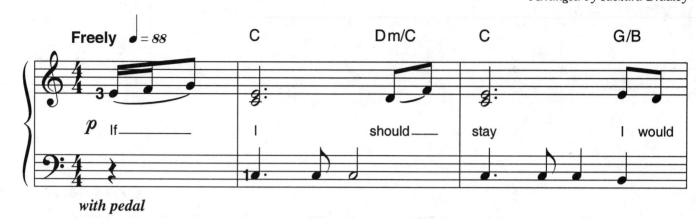

with pedal

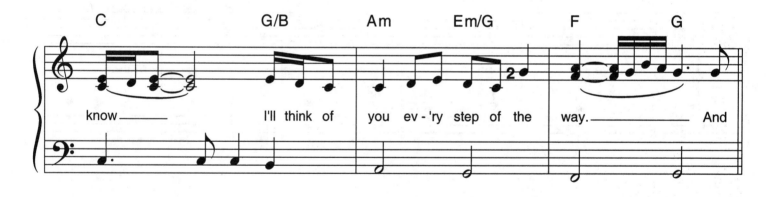

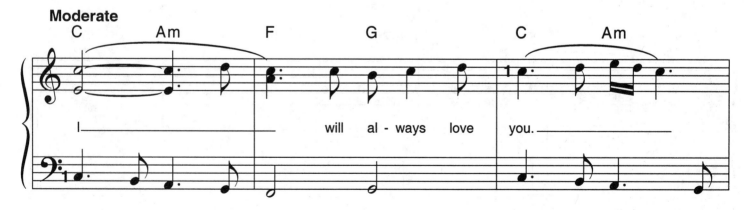

I Will Always Love You - 4 - 1

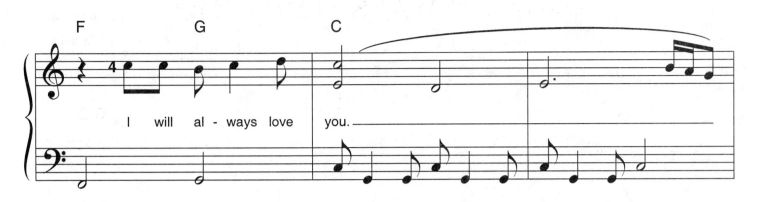

I will al - ways love you. _____

You, my dar - ling, you. Hmm. _____ Bit - ter

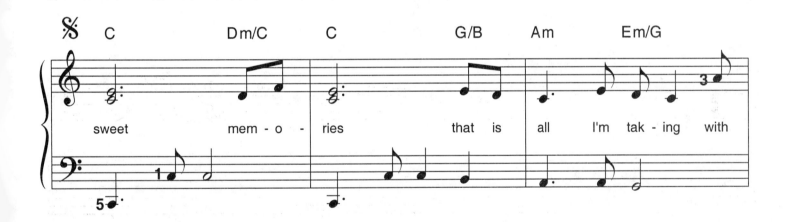

sweet mem - o - ries that is all I'm tak - ing with

me. _____ So good - bye. _____ Please, _____

116

*Coda*

love. And

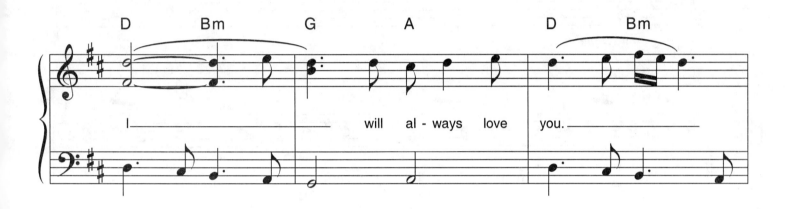

I will al - ways love you.

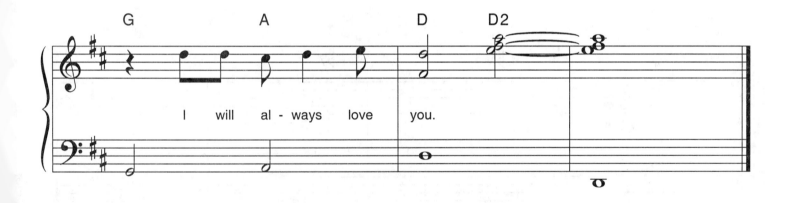

I will al - ways love you.

*Verse 3:*
I hope life treats you kind
And I hope you have all you've dreamed of.
And I wish to you, joy and happiness.
But above all this, I wish you love.

# LOVE MAKES THE WORLD GO 'ROUND

From the Broadway Musical *Carnival*

Words and Music by
BOB MERRILL
*Arranged by Richard Bradley*

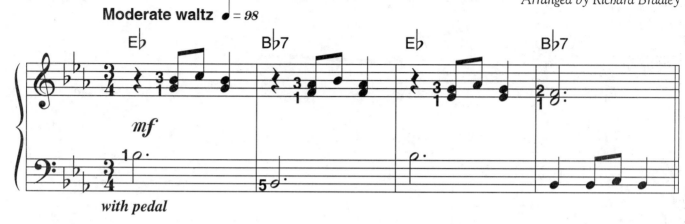

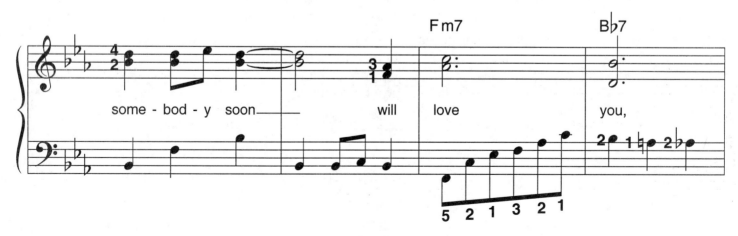

Love Makes The World Go 'Round - 2 - 1

# SUMMERTIME

From the Folk Opera *Porgy and Bess*

Music by GEORGE GERSHWIN
Lyric by IRA GERSHWIN,
DU BOIS and DOROTHY HEYWARD
Arranged by Richard Bradley

Summertime - 4 - 1

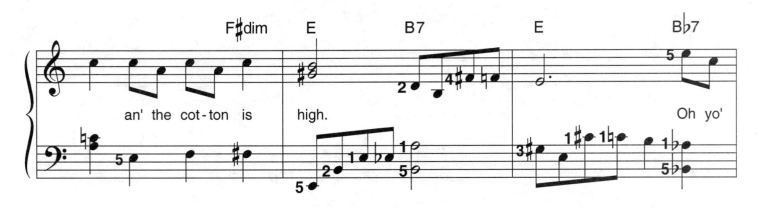

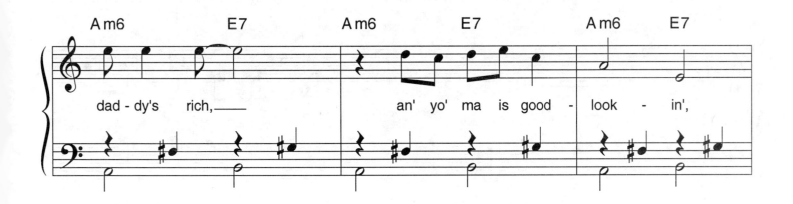

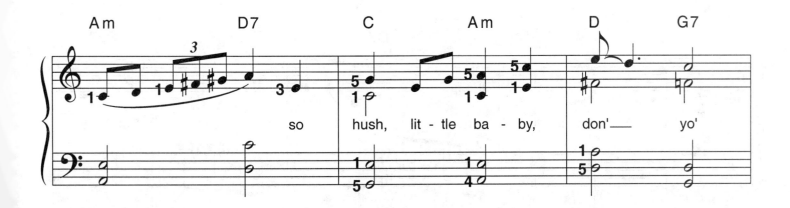

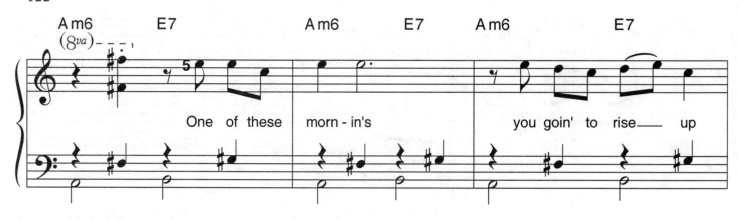

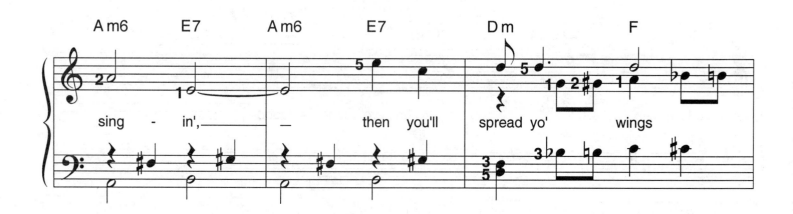

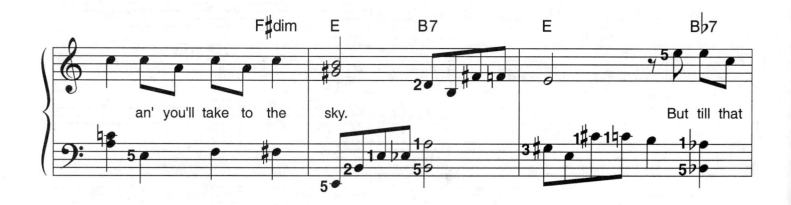

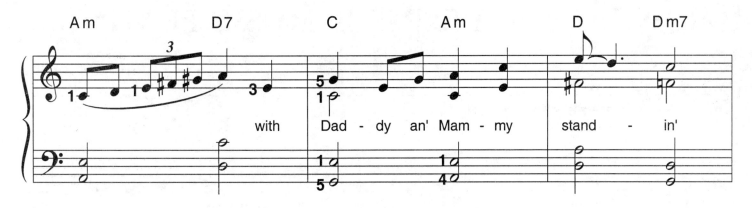

with Dad - dy an' Mam - my stand - in'

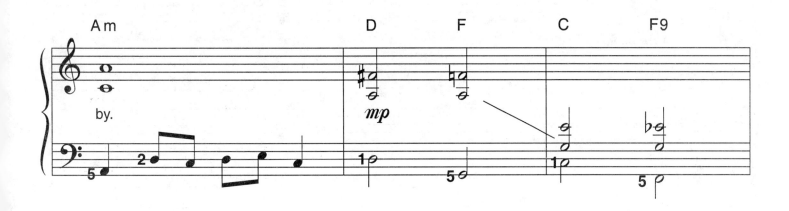

by.

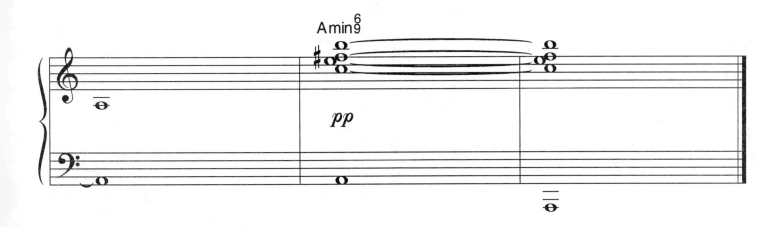

Summertime - 4 - 4

# HOW DO YOU KEEP THE MUSIC PLAYING?

Words by
ALAN and MARILYN BERGMAN

Music by
MICHEL LEGRAND

# ALMOST LIKE BEING IN LOVE

From the Broadway Musical *Brigadoon*

Lyrics by ALAN J. LERNER
Music by FREDERICK LOEWE
Arranged by Richard Bradley

Almost Like Being In Love - 3 - 1

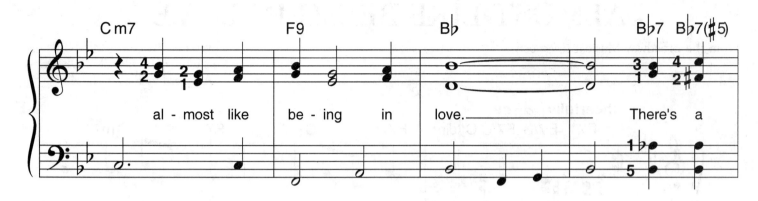

al - most like be - ing in love._____ There's a

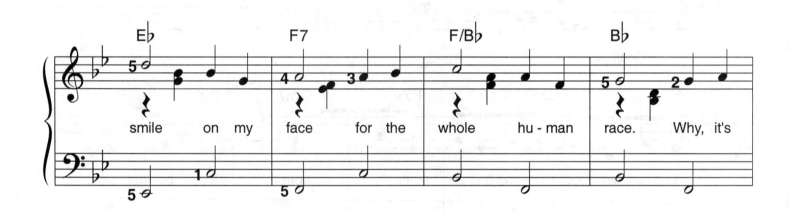

smile on my face for the whole hu - man race. Why, it's

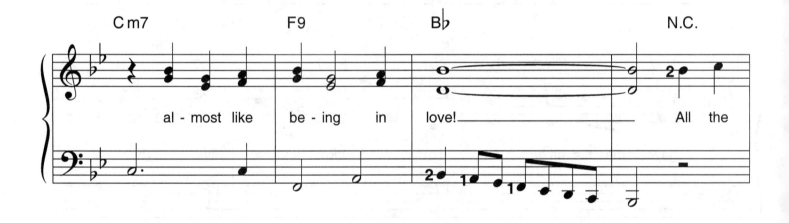

al - most like be - ing in love!_____ All the

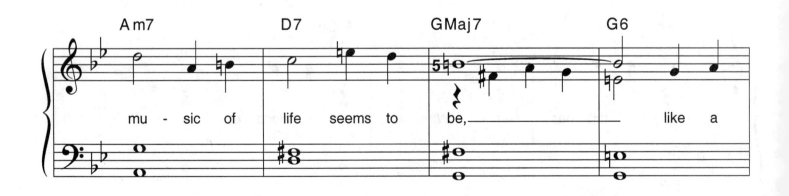

mu - sic of life seems to be,_____ like a

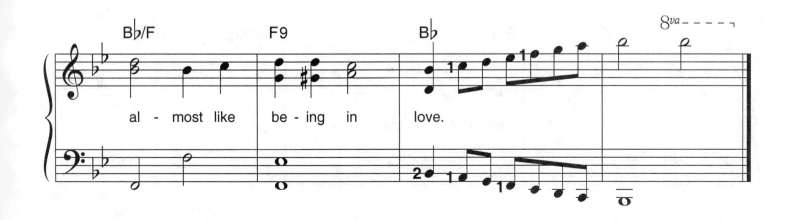

# THAT'S WHAT FRIENDS ARE FOR

Words and Music by
BURT BACHARACH and
CAROLE BAYER SAGER
*Arranged by Richard Bradley*

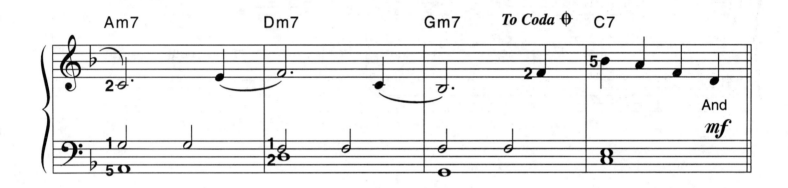

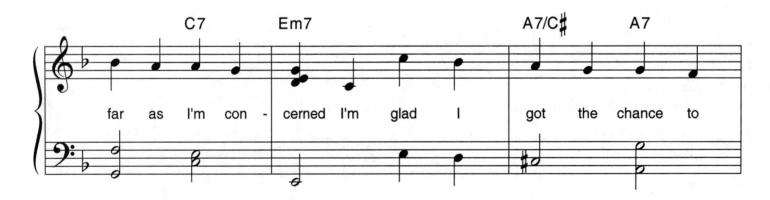

That's What Friends Are For - 3 - 1

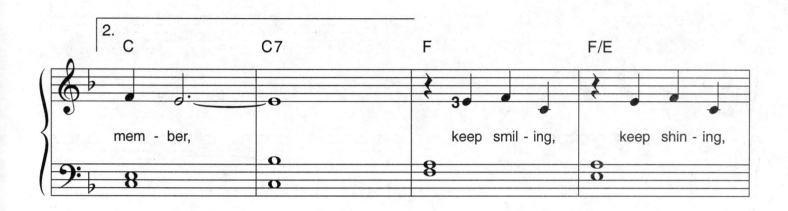

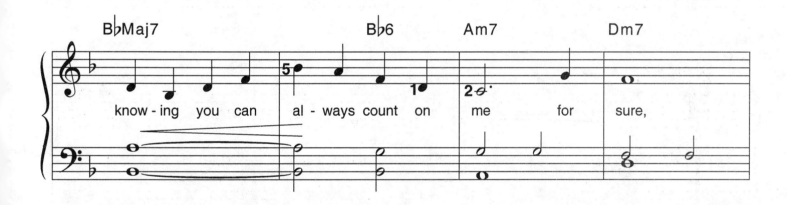

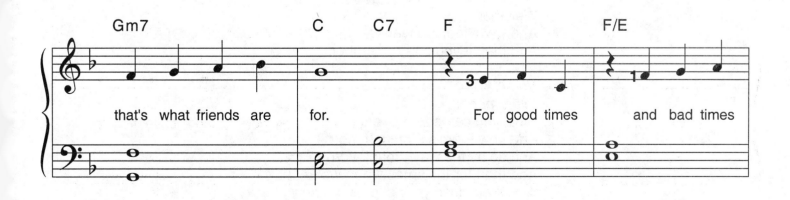

That's What Friends Are For - 3 - 2

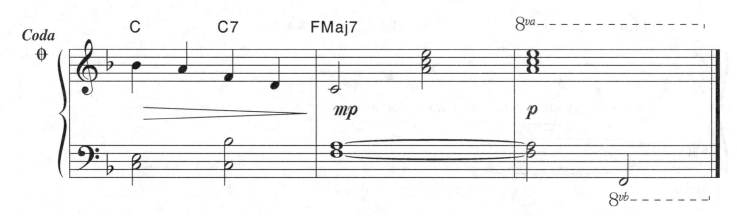

*Verse 2*:
And if I should ever go away,
Well then close your eyes
And try to feel the way we do today
And then if you can remember,

*Verse 3*:
*Instrumental*
Well, you came and opened me
And now there's so much more I see.
And so by the way I thank you.
And then for the times when we're apart,
Well then close your eyes and know
These words are coming from my heart.

# HEY, LOOK ME OVER

From the Broadway Musical *Wildcat*

Music by CY COLEMAN
Lyrics by CAROLYN LEIGH
*Arranged by Richard Bradley*

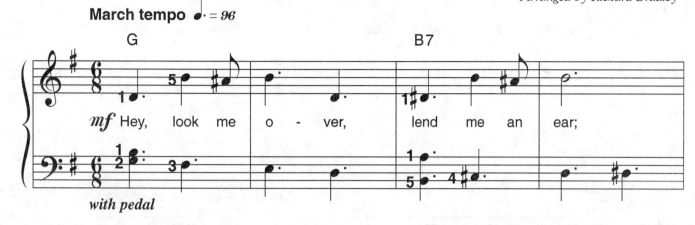

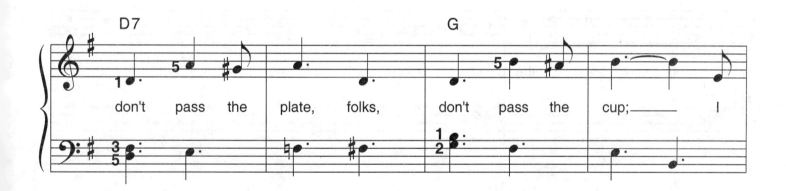

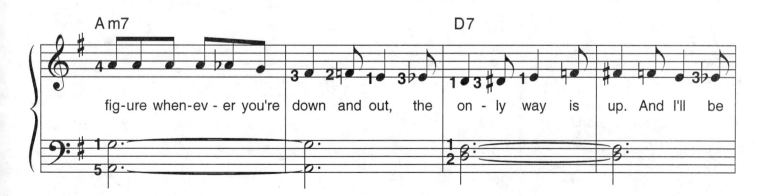

Hey, Look Me Over - 3 - 1

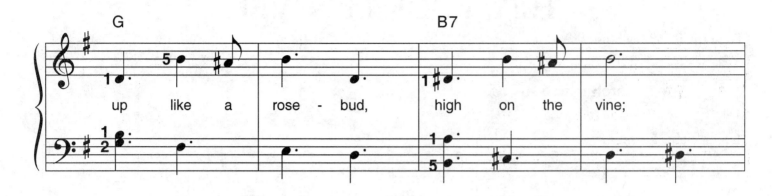

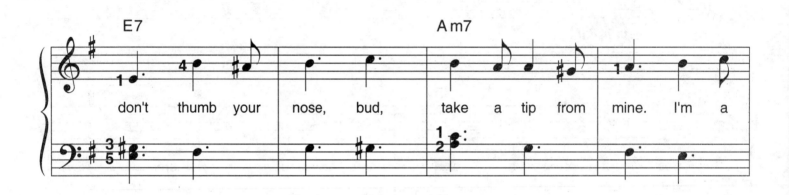

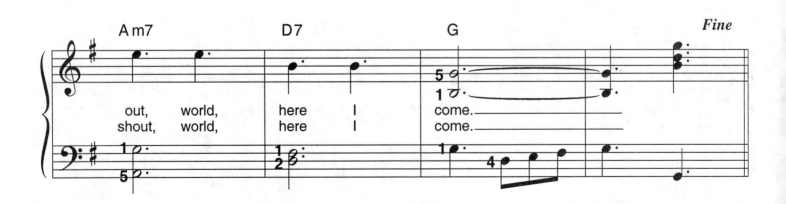

**G**

No - bod - y in the world was ev - er with - out a pray'r;

**F**

how can you win the world, if no - bod - y knows you're there.

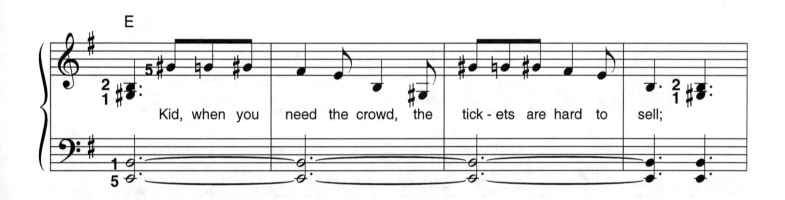

**E**

Kid, when you need the crowd, the tick - ets are hard to sell;

**D7**

*D.C. al Fine*

still you can lead the crowd, if you can get up and yell:

Hey, Look Me Over - 3 - 3

# TEN CENTS A DANCE

From the Broadway Musical *Simple Simon*

Words by LORENZ HART
Music by RICHARD RODGERS
*Arranged by Richard Bradley*

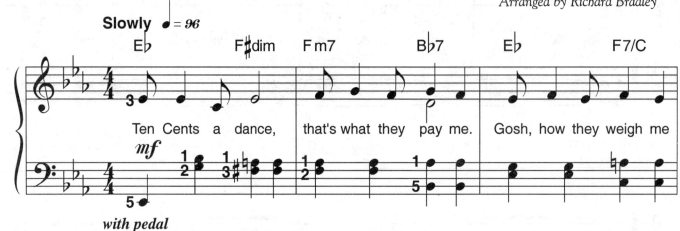

Ten Cents a dance, that's what they pay me. Gosh, how they weigh me

*with pedal*

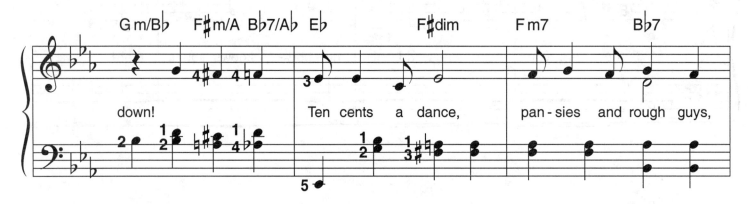

down! Ten cents a dance, pan-sies and rough guys,

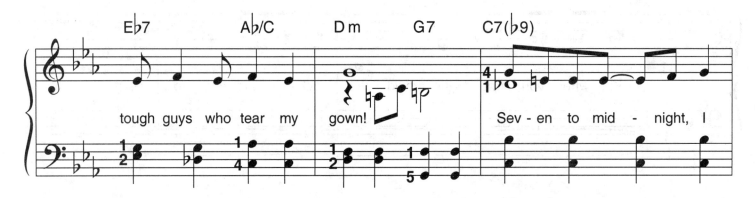

tough guys who tear my gown! Sev-en to mid-night, I

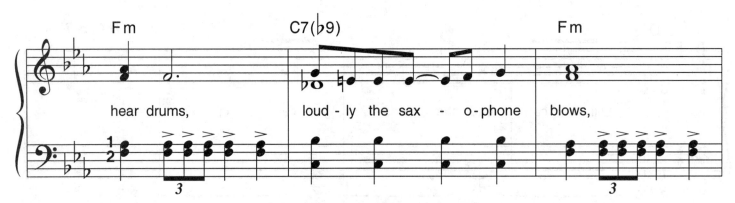

hear drums, loud-ly the sax-o-phone blows,

Ten Cents A Dance - 4 - 1

trum - pets are tear - ing my ear - drums. Cus - tom - ers crush my

toes. Some - times I think I've found my he - ro,

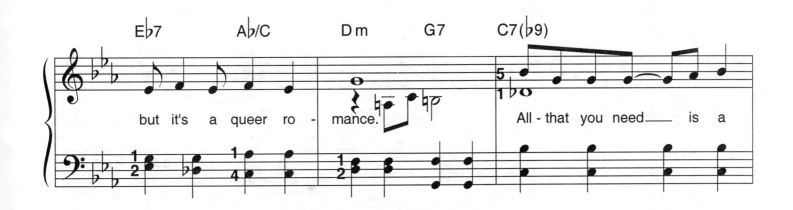

but it's a queer ro - mance. All - that you need____ is a

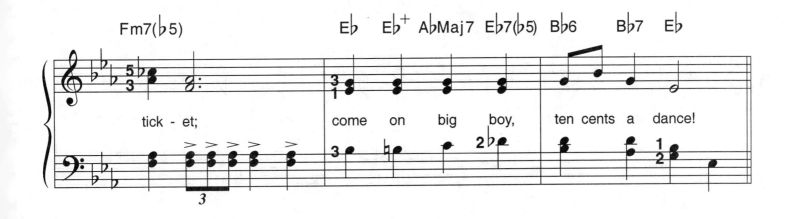

tick - et; come on big boy, ten cents a dance!

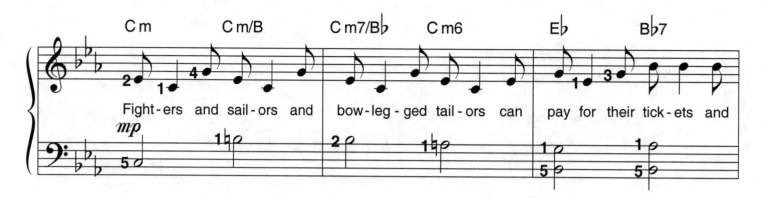

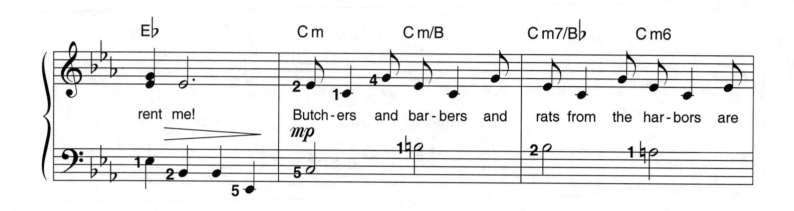

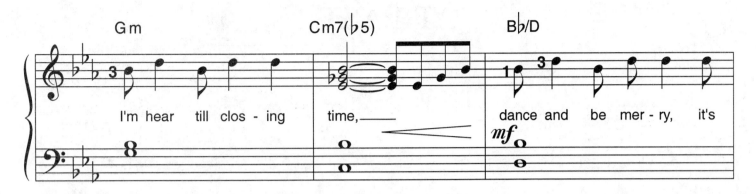

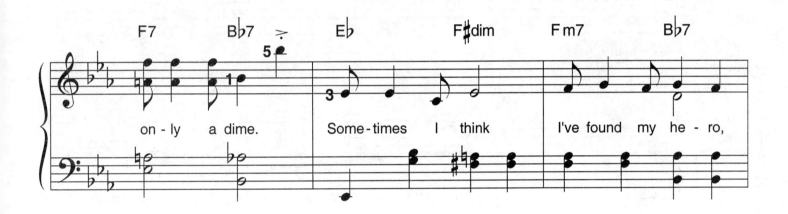

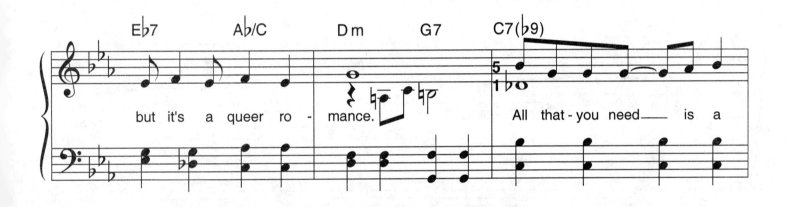

Ten Cents A Dance - 4 - 4

# AT LAST

Lyric by
**MACK GORDON**

Music by
**HARRY WARREN**
*Arranged by Richard Bradley*

At Last - 3 - 1

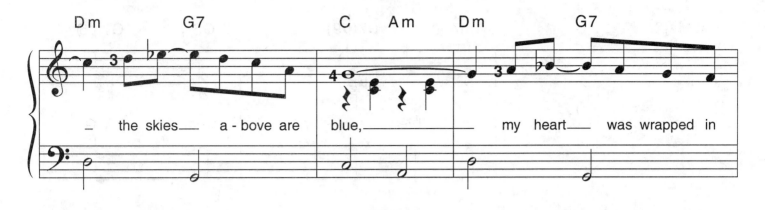

the skies— a-bove are blue,— my heart— was wrapped in

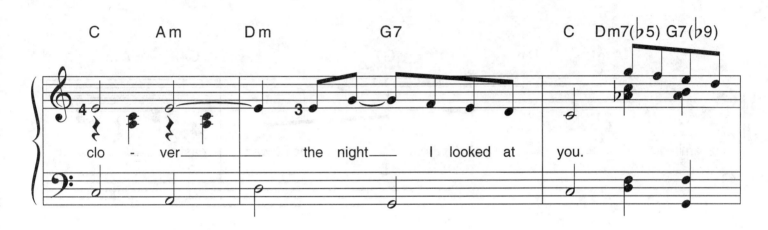

clo - ver— the night— I looked at you.

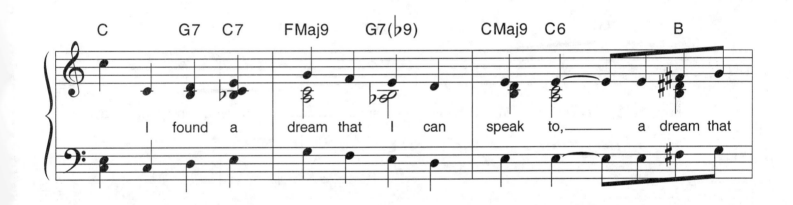

I found a dream that I can speak to,— a dream that

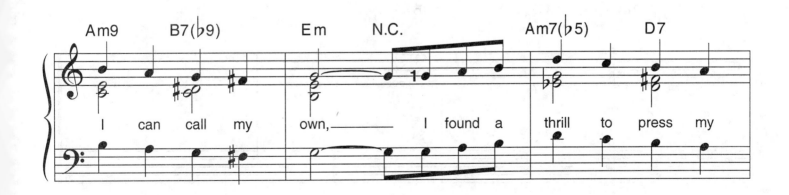

I can call my own,— I found a thrill to press my

At Last - 3 - 2

142

GMaj7　　　　C　　　　Am7　　　D7(♭9)　　　　　G6　　　G7(♯5)

cheek　to,　　a　　thrill　I've　nev - er　　　known.　　　You

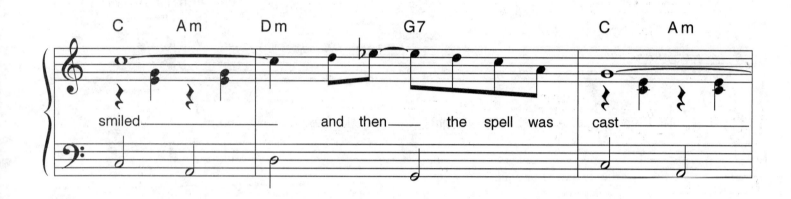

C　　Am　　　Dm　　　　　G7　　　　　　C　　　Am

smiled＿＿＿　　　　　　　　and then＿＿　the　spell　was　cast＿＿＿

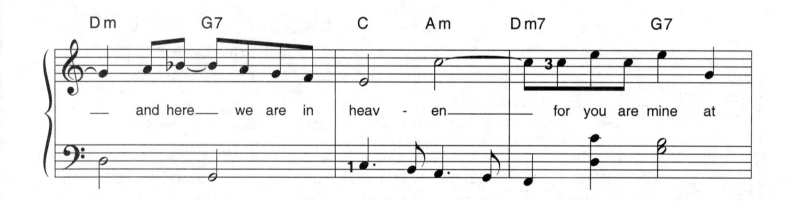

Dm　　　　G7　　　　　C　　Am　　　Dm7　　　　G7

＿　and here＿　we　are　in　heav - en＿＿＿＿　for　you　are　mine　at

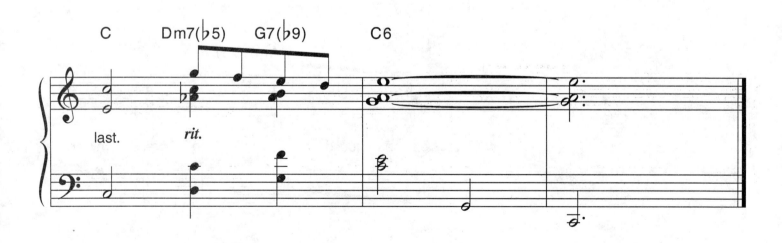

C　　Dm7(♭5)　G7(♭9)　　C6

last.　　rit.

# ON GREEN DOLPHIN STREET
*(Instrumental version)*

Lyrics by
NED WASHINGTON

Music by
BRONISLAU KAPER
*Arranged by Richard Bradley*

On Green Dolphin Street - 3 - 1

**LYRICS**
Lover, one lovely day.
Love came, planning to stay.
Green Dolphin Street supplied the setting
The setting for nights beyond forgetting.
And through these moments apart
Mem'ries live in my heart.
When I recall the love I found on,
I could kiss the ground
On Green Dolphin Street.

# TARA THEME

From the Motion Picture *Gone With the Wind*

Music by
MAX STEINER
*Arranged by Richard Bradley*

Tara Theme - 2 - 1

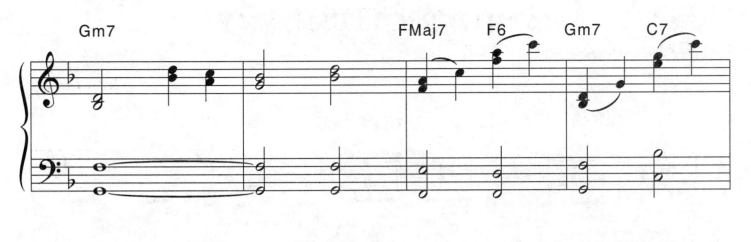

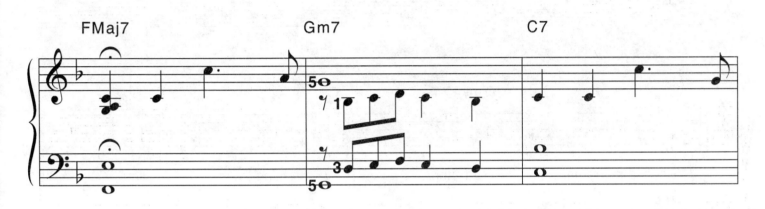

# CORNER OF THE SKY

From the Broadway Musical *Pippin*

Words and Music by
STEPHEN SCHWARTZ
Arranged by Richard Bradley

Corner Of The Sky - 4 - 1

*Corner Of The Sky - 4 - 2*

got to find my cor - ner of the

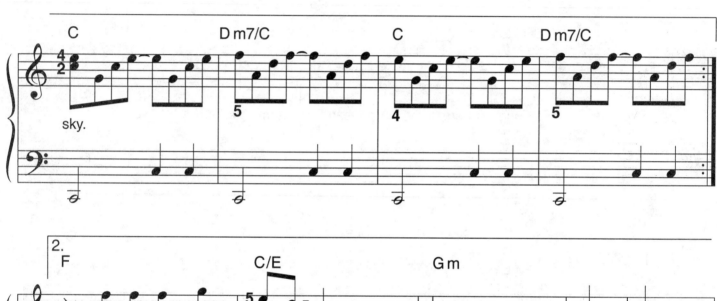

sky.

got to find my cor - ner of the

sky. And

got to find my cor - ner of the

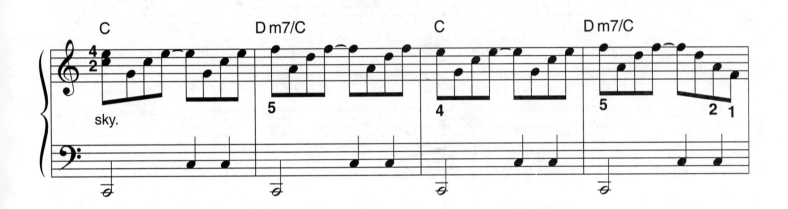

sky.

*Verse 2:*
Every man has his daydreams,
Every man has his goal,
People like the way dreams
Have of sticking to the soul.
Rain comes after thunder,
Winter comes after fall.
Sometimes I think I'm not after
Anything at all.

*Verse 3:*
And maybe some misty day,
You'll waken to find me gone.
And far away you'll hear me
Singing to the dawn.
And you'll wonder if I'm happy there
A little more than I've been.
And the answer will come back to you
Like laughter on the wind.

# ANYTHING GOES

From the Broadway Musical *Anything Goes*

Words and Music by
COLE PORTER
*Arranged by Richard Bradley*

**Moderately** ♩ = 124

*with pedal*

*Anything Goes - 3 - 1*

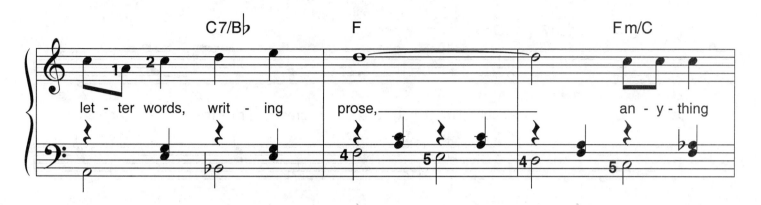

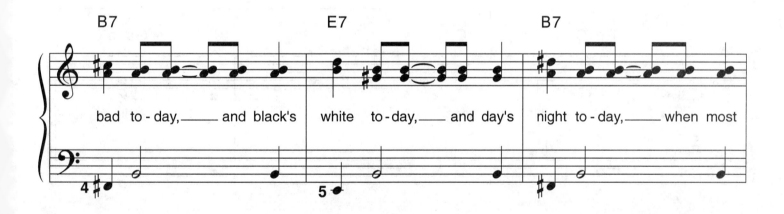

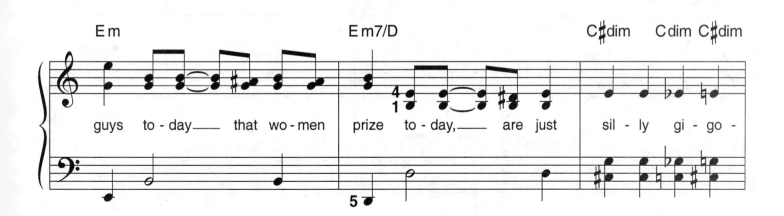

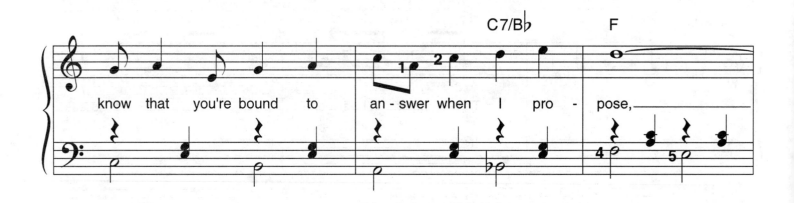

# TOOT, TOOT, TOOTSIE!

By GUS KAHN, ERNIE ERDMAN,
DAN RUSSO and TED FIORITO
*Arranged by Richard Bradley*

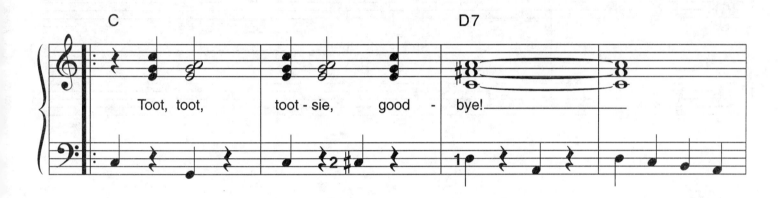

Toot, toot, toot - sie, good - bye!

Toot, toot, toot - sie don't cry.

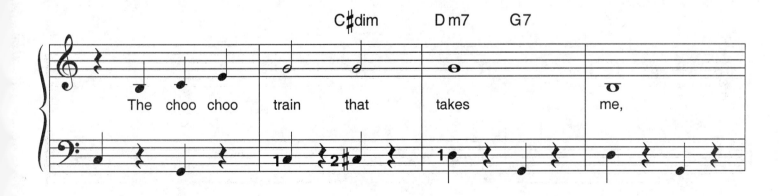

The choo choo train that takes me,

Toot, Toot, Tootsie - 3 - 1

157

you don't get a let - ter then you'll know I'm in jail.

*rit.*

Toot, toot,     toot - sie,     don't     cry,

*a tempo*

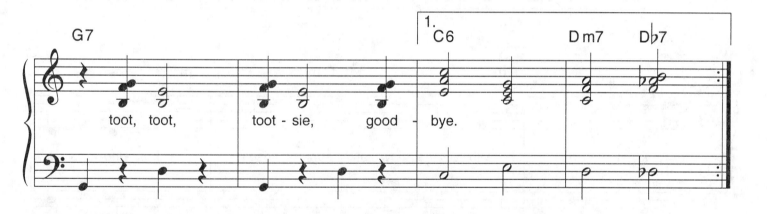

toot, toot,     toot - sie,     good - bye.

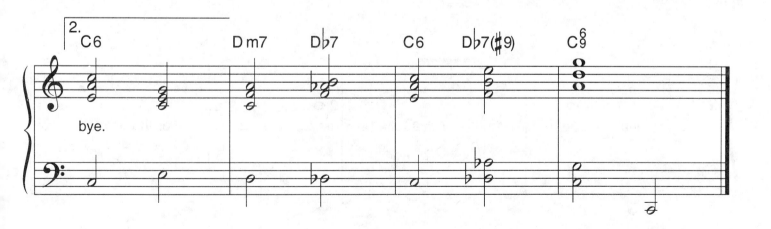

bye.

Toot, Toot, Tootsie - 3 - 3

# SOFTLY, AS IN A MORNING SUNRISE

Words by
OSCAR HAMMERSTEIN II

Music by
SIGMUND ROMBERG

*Softly, As In A Morning Sunrise - 2 - 1*

thrill love, and lift you high to heav - en,_____ are the pas-sions that

kill love, and let you fall to hell! So ends each sto - ry.

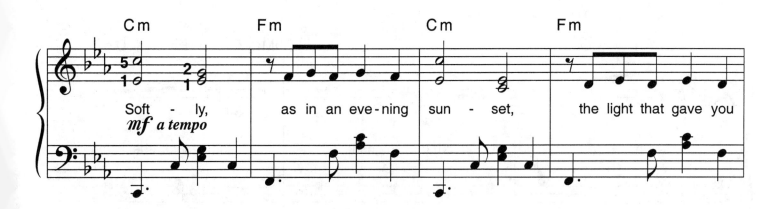

Soft - ly, as in an eve-ning sun - set, the light that gave you

glo - ry will take it all a - way.

# ONCE UPON A TIME

From the Broadway Musical *All American*

Lyrics by LEE ADAMS
Music by CHARLES STROUSE
*Arranged by Richard Bradley*

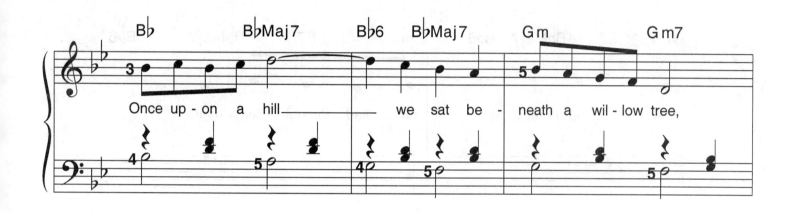

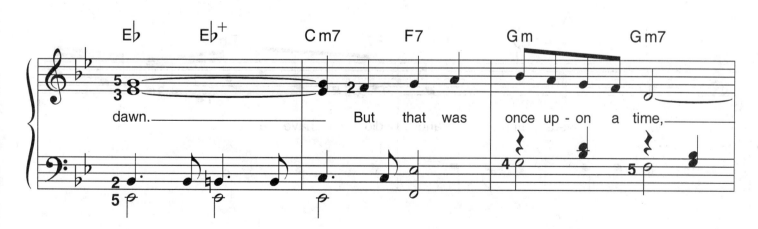

Once Upon A Time - 4 - 2

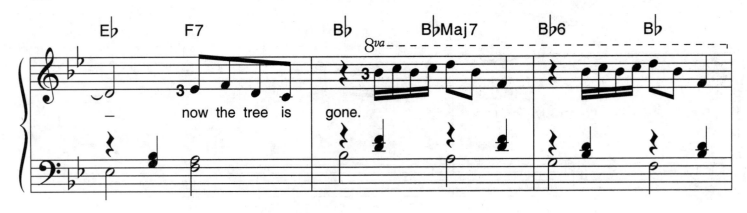

now the tree is gone.

How the breeze ruf - fled through her hair,

how we al - ways laughed as tho' to - mor - row was - n't there.

We were young and did - n't have a care.

# I'VE GOTTA BE ME

From the Broadway Musical *Golden Rainbow*

Music and Lyrics by
WALTER MARKS
Arranged by Richard Bradley

*I've Gotta Be Me - 4 - 1*

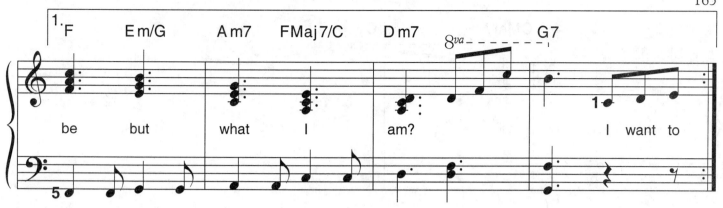

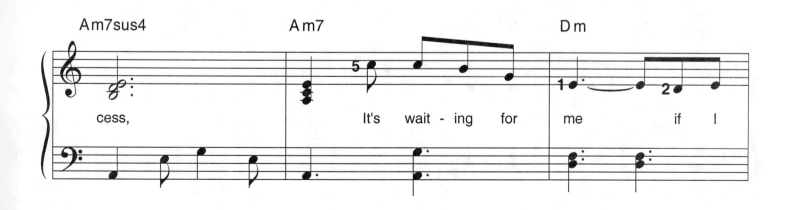

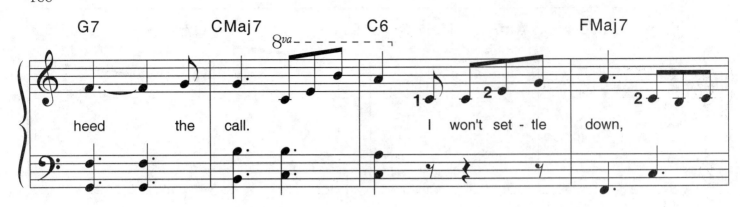

heed the call. I won't set - tle down,

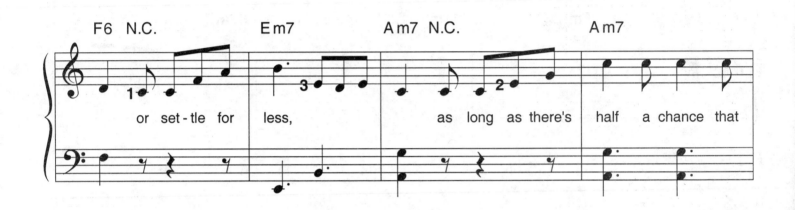

or set - tle for less, as long as there's half a chance that

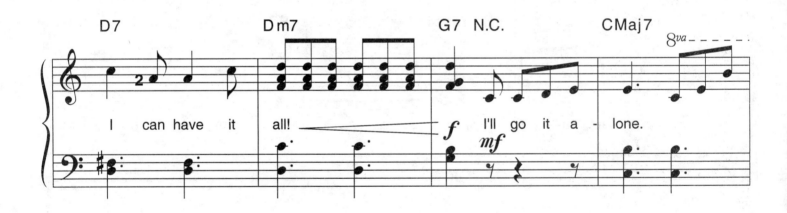

I can have it all! I'll go it a - lone.

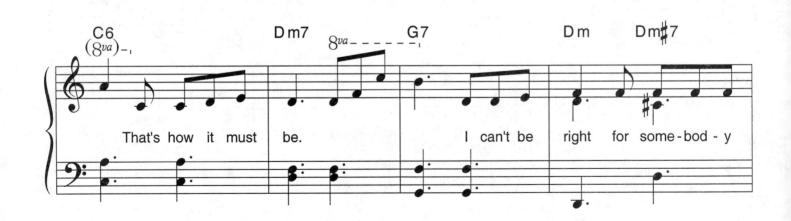

That's how it must be. I can't be right for some - bod - y

Verse 2:
I want to live! Not merely survive!
And I won't give up this dream of life
That keeps me alive!
I've gotta be me! I've gotta be me!
The dream that I see makes me what I am!

# HEART

From the Broadway Musical *Damn Yankees*

Words and Music by
RICHARD ADLER and JERRY ROSS
*Arranged by Richard Bradley*

Heart - 3 - 1

noth-in's half as bad as it may ap-pear,___ wait-'ll next year___ and

hope. When your luck is bat-tin' ze-ro,___

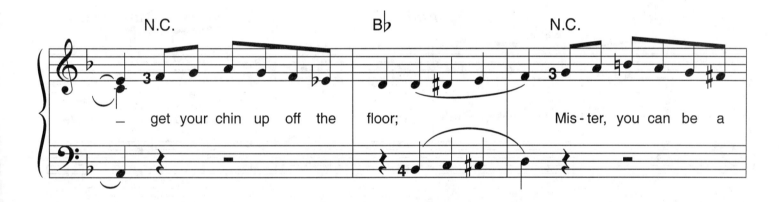

— get your chin up off the floor; Mis-ter, you can be a

he-ro, you can o-pen an-y door, there's noth-in' to it, but to

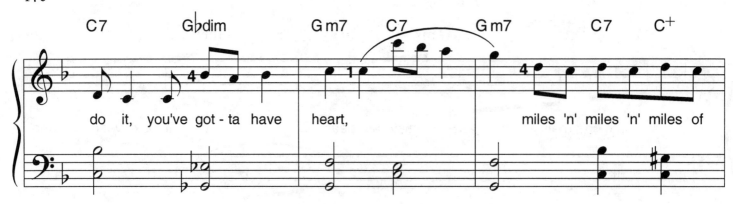

do it, you've got - ta have heart, miles 'n' miles 'n' miles of

heart. Oh, it's fine to be a gen - ius of course,_____ but

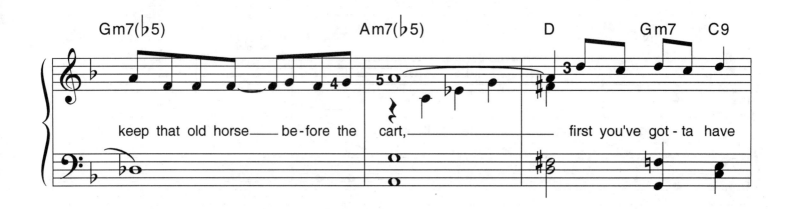

keep that old horse_____ be - fore the cart,_____ first you've got - ta have

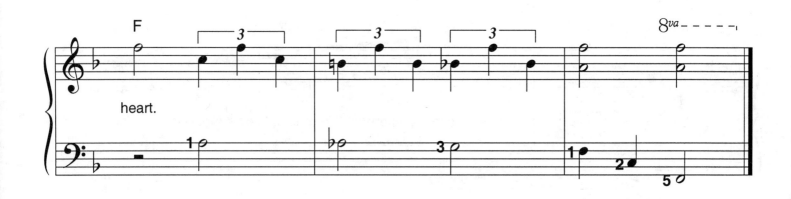

heart.

# BIG SPENDER

From the Broadway Musical *Sweet Charity*

Music by CY COLEMAN
Lyrics by DOROTHY FIELDS
*Arranged by Richard Bradley*

**Moderately, with a beat** ♩ = 116

The min - ute you

walked in the joint, I could see you were a

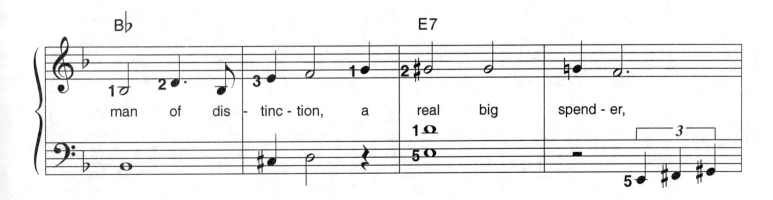

man of dis - tinc - tion, a real big spend - er,

Big Spender - 5 - 1

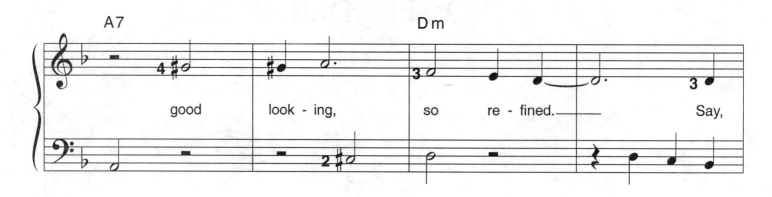

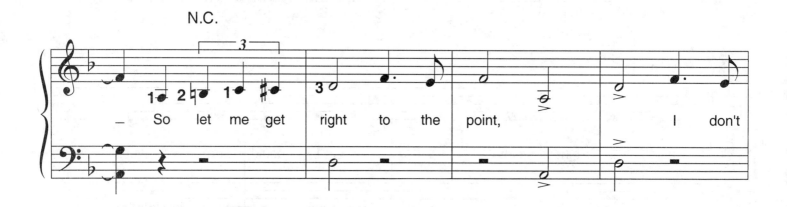

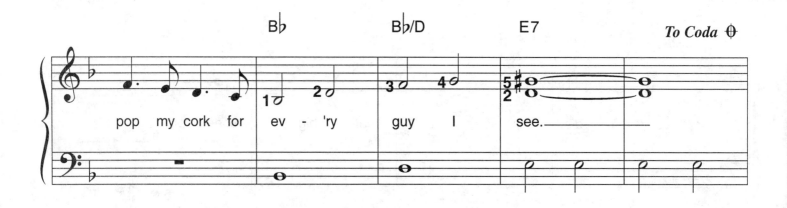

# SUNRISE, SUNSET

From the Broadway Musical *Fiddler On The Roof*

Lyrics by SHELDON HARNICK
Music by JERRY BOCK
*Arranged by Richard Bradley*

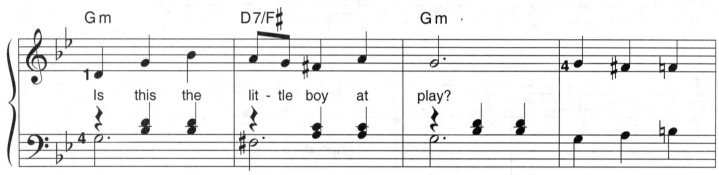

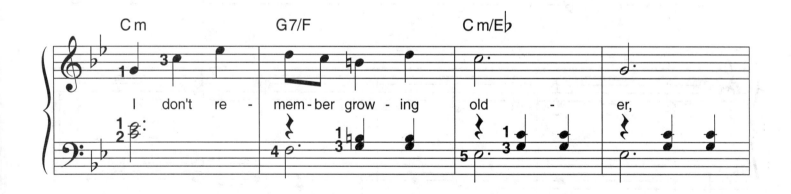

Sunrise, Sunset - 4 - 1

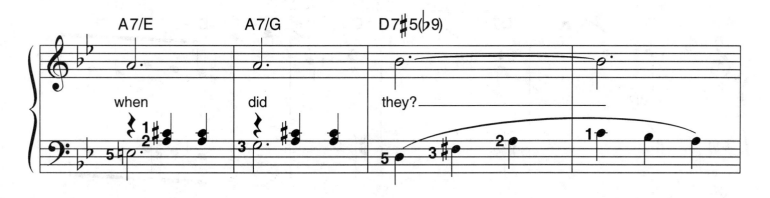

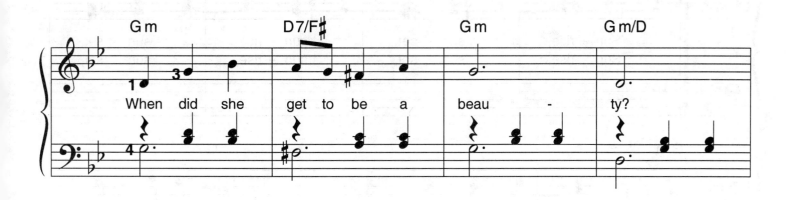

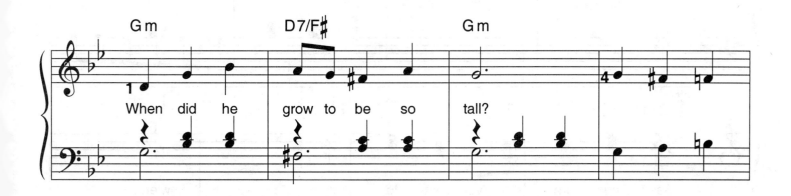

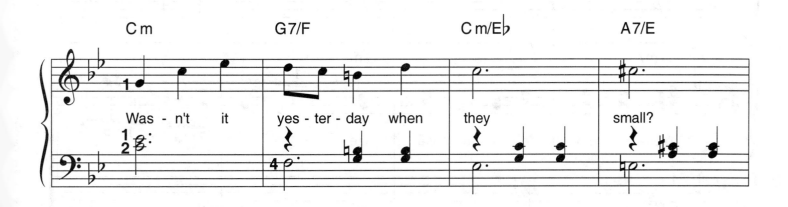

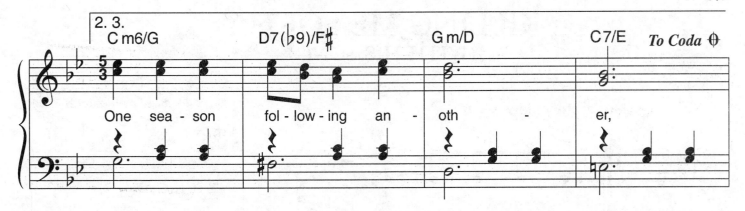

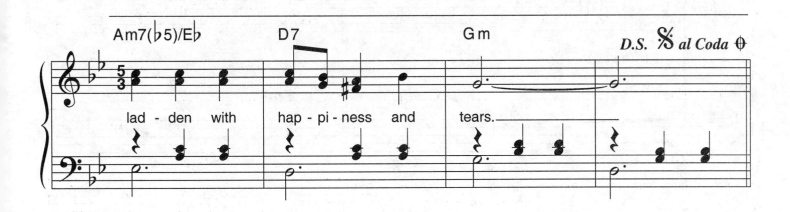

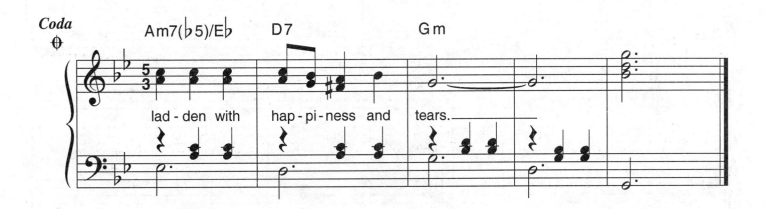

*Verse 2:*
Now is the little boy a bridegroom?
Now is the little girl a bride?
Under the canopy I see them, side by side.
Place the gold ring around her finger,
Share the sweet wine and break the glass;
Soon the full circle will have come to pass.

# KILLING ME SOFTLY
## (WITH HIS SONG)

Words by
NORMAN GIMBEL

Music by
CHARLES FOX
*Arranged by Richard Bradley*

# BIDIN' MY TIME

From the Broadway Musicals *Girl Crazy* and *Crazy For You*

Words by IRA GERSHWIN
Music by GEORGE GERSHWIN
*Arranged by Richard Bradley*

Bidin' My Time - 3 - 1

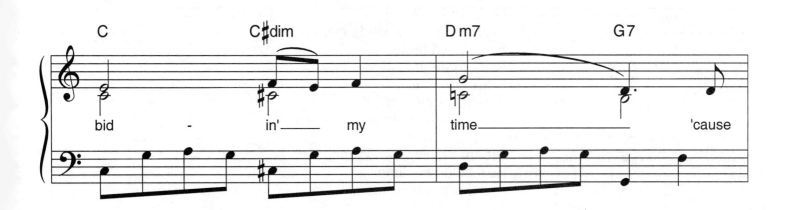

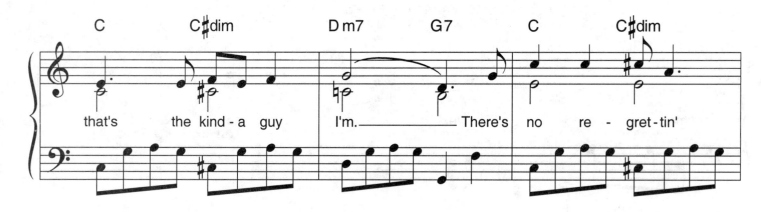

that's    the kind-a guy    I'm._____There's    no    re - gret-tin'

when    I'm    set-tin'    bid  -  in'___ my    time.

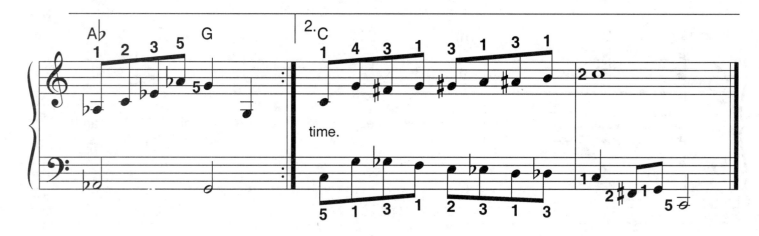

time.

*Verse 2:*
I'm bidin' my time;
'Cause that's the kinda guy I'm,
Beginin' on a Monday
Right through Sunday,
Bidin' my time.
Give me, give me,
Glass that's bright and twinkles.
Let me, let me,
Dream like Rip Van Winkle.
He's bided his time
And that's the winkle guy I'm,
Chasin' way flies,
How the day flies,
Bidin' my time.

# I'VE GOT YOUR NUMBER

From the Broadway Musical *Little Me*

Music by CY COLEMAN
Lyrics by CAROLYN LEIGH
*Arranged by Richard Bradley*

I've got your num - ber,___ I know you in - side___ out,

you ain't no Ea - gle___ Scout, you're all at sea!

Oh, yes, you'll brag a lot,___ wave your own___ flag a lot,___

*I've Got Your Number - 3 - 1*

but your un - sure a lot,____ you're a lot____ like me. Oh,

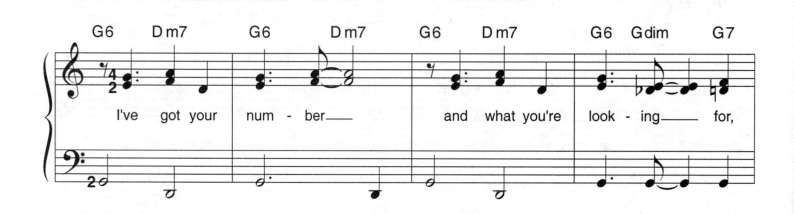

I've got your num - ber____ and what you're look - ing____ for,

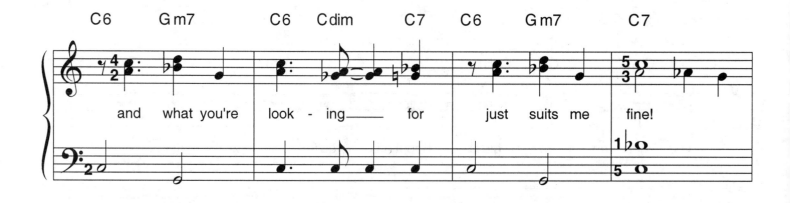

and what you're look - ing____ for just suits me fine!

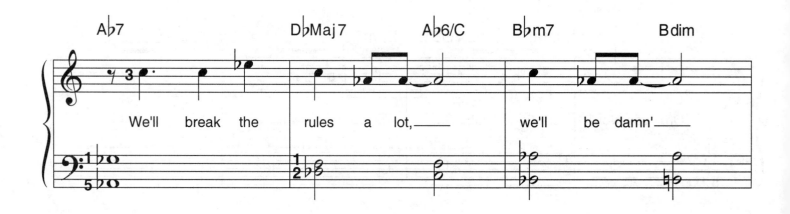

We'll break the rules a lot,____ we'll be damn'____

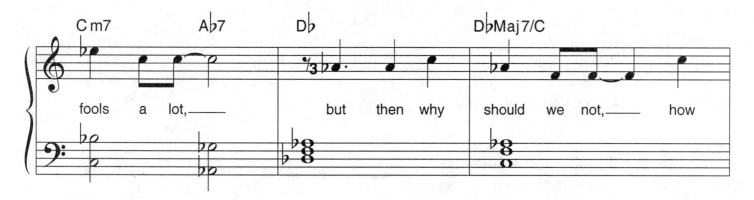

fools a lot,_____ but then why should we not,_____ how

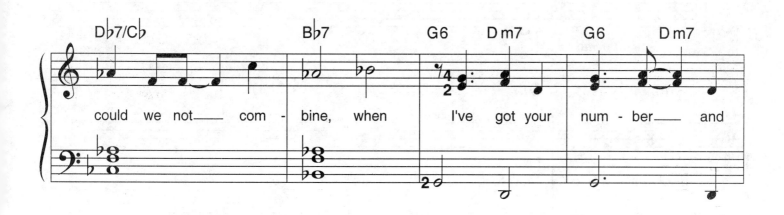

could we not____ com - bine, when I've got your num - ber____ and

I've got the glow you've____ got, I've got your num - ber____ and

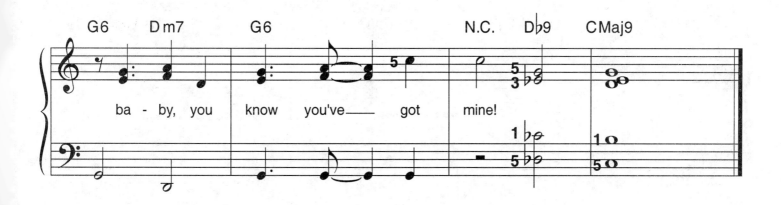

ba - by, you know you've____ got mine!

# TOMORROW

From the Broadway Musical *Annie*

Lyrics by MARTIN CHARNIN
Music by CHARLES STROUSE
*Arranged by Richard Bradley*

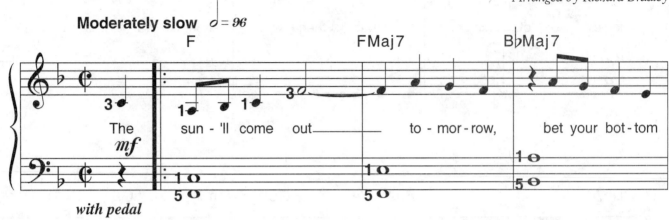

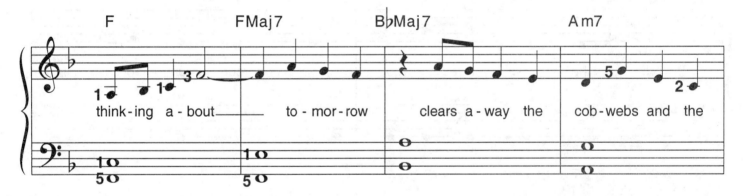

Tomorrow - 4 - 1

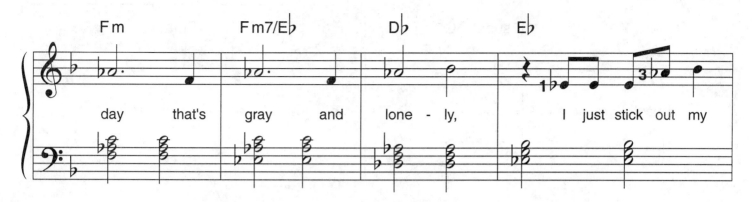

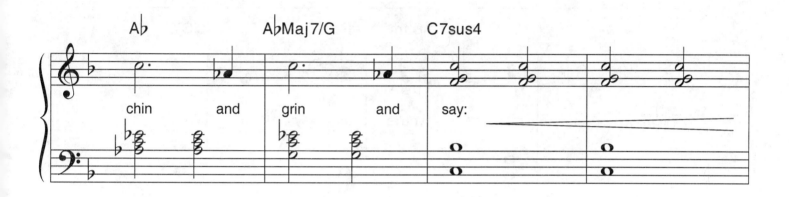

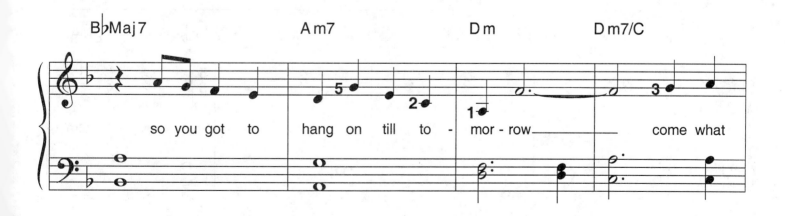

Tomorrow - 4 - 2

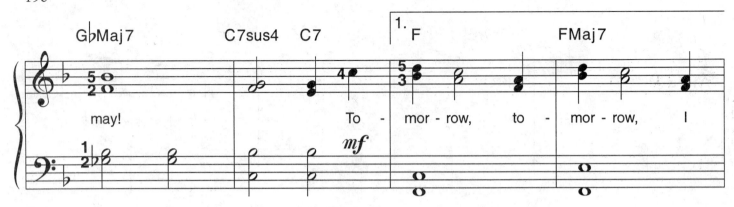

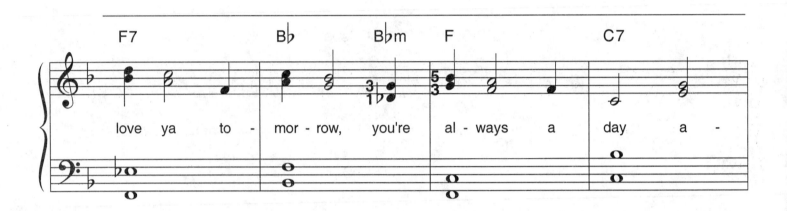

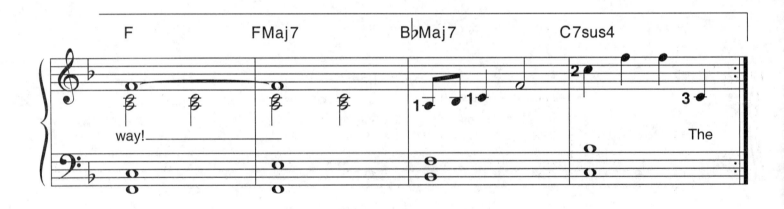

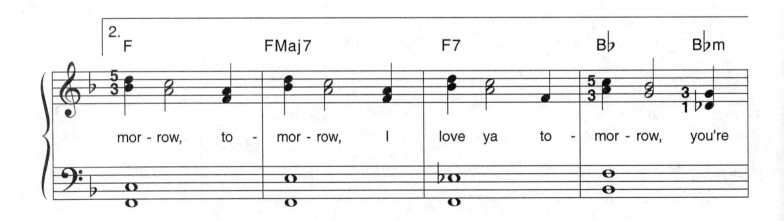

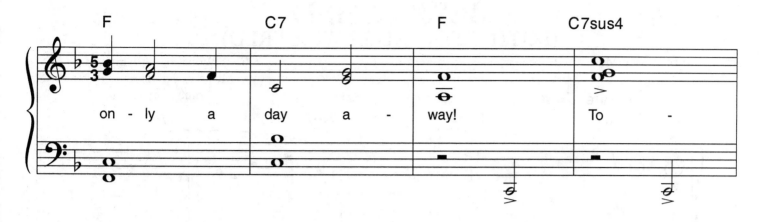

on - ly a day a - way! To -

mor - row, to - mor - row, I love ya to - mor - row, you're

on - ly a day a - way!

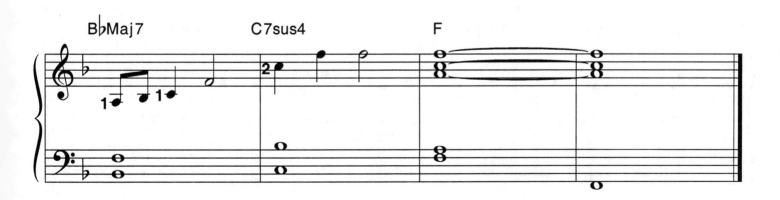

# BEWITCHED
## (BOTHERED AND BEWILDERED)

From the Broadway Musical *Pal Joey*

Words by LORENZ HART
Music by RICHARD RODGERS
*Arranged by Richard Bradley*

He's a fool and don't I know it, but a fool can have his charms;

I'm in love and don't I show it, like a babe in arms.

Love's the same old sad sen-sa-tion, late-ly I've not slept a wink,

Bewitched - 4 - 1

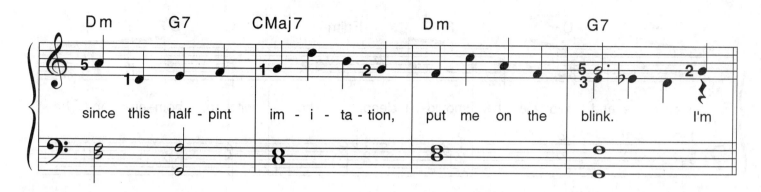

since this half - pint im - i - ta - tion, put me on the blink. I'm

wild a - gain, be - guiled a - gain, a sim - per - ing, whim - per - ing

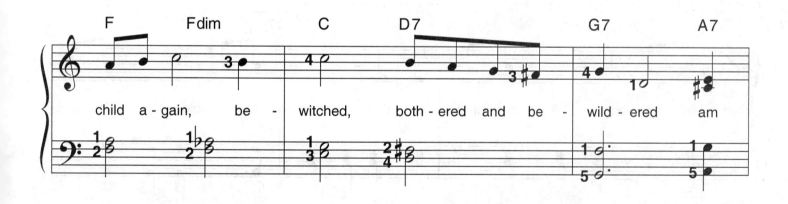

child a - gain, be - witched, both - ered and be - wild - ered am

I. Could-n't sleep, and would-n't sleep, when

love came and told me I should-n't sleep, be - witched, both-ered and be -

wild - ered am I.

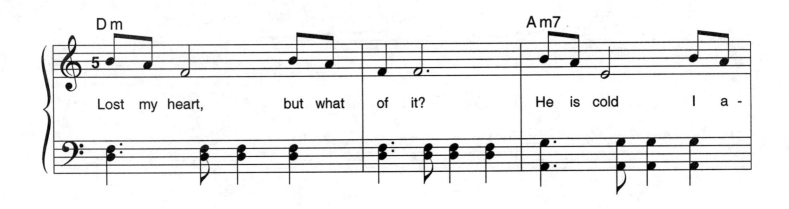

Lost my heart, but what of it? He is cold I a -

gree. He can laugh, but I love it,_____ al-though the

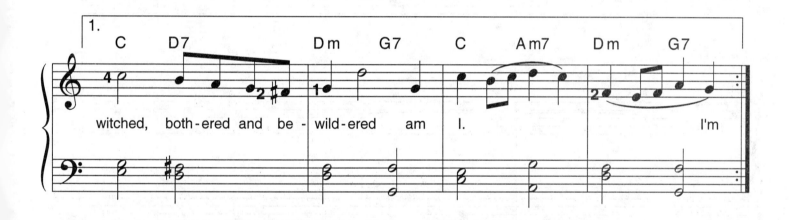

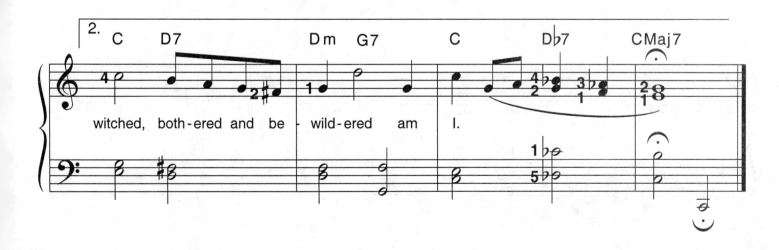

Bewitched - 4 - 4

# CARAVAN

By
DUKE ELLINGTON,
JUAN TIXOL and IRVING MILLS
*Arranged by Richard Bradley*

Caravan - 4 - 1

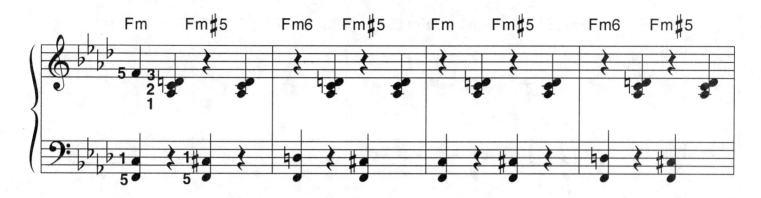

*To Coda* ✪

Caravan - 4 - 2

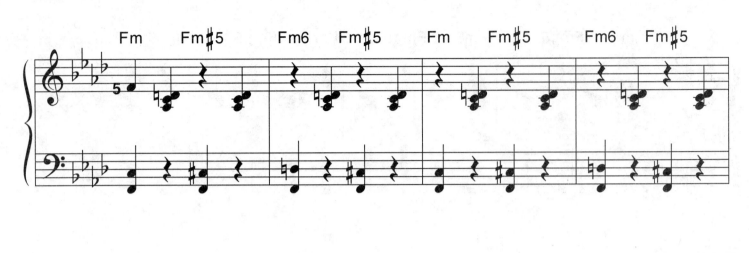

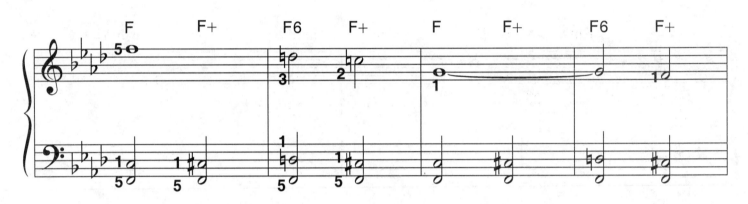

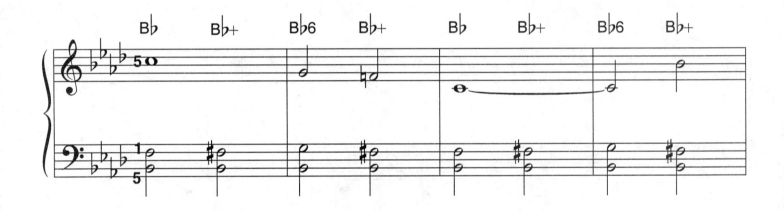

Caravan - 4 - 4

# I GOT RHYTHM

From the Broadway Musicals *Girl Crazy* and *Crazy For You*

Words by IRA GERSHWIN
Music by GEORGE GERSHWIN
*Arranged by Richard Bradley*

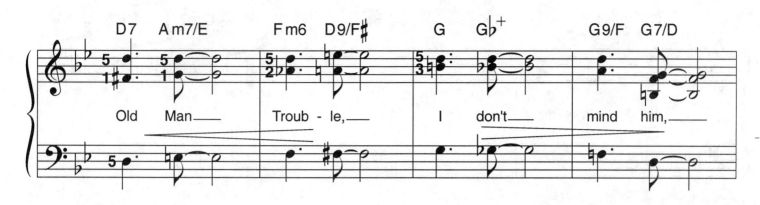

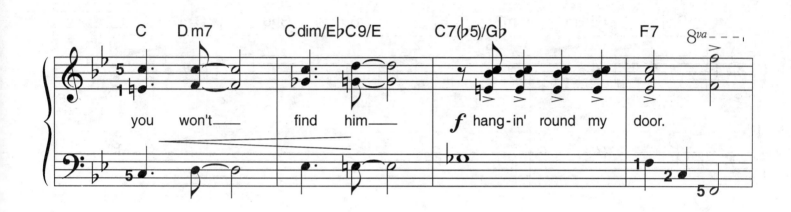

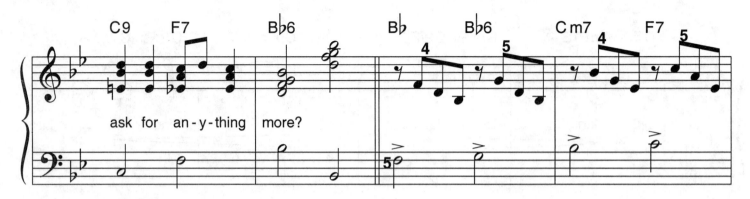

ask for an-y-thing more?

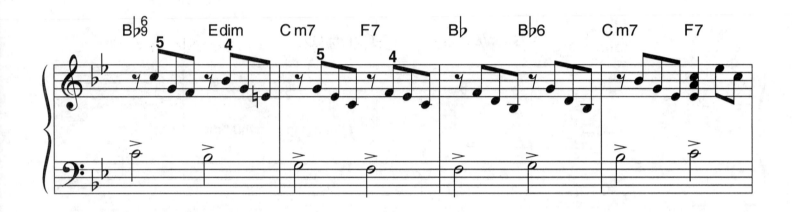

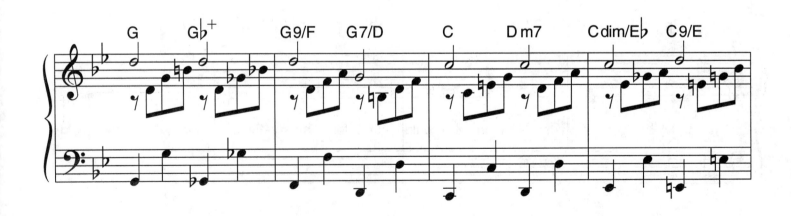

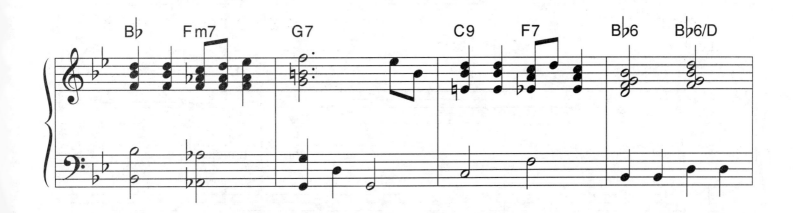

I Got Rhythm - 4 - 4

# STRIKE UP THE BAND

From the Broadway Musical *Strike Up The Band*

Words by IRA GERSHWIN
Music by GEORGE GERSHWIN
*Arranged by Richard Bradley*

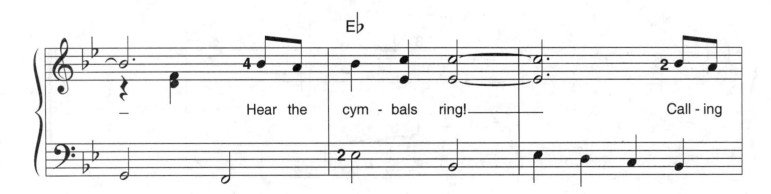

Strike Up The Band - 3 - 1

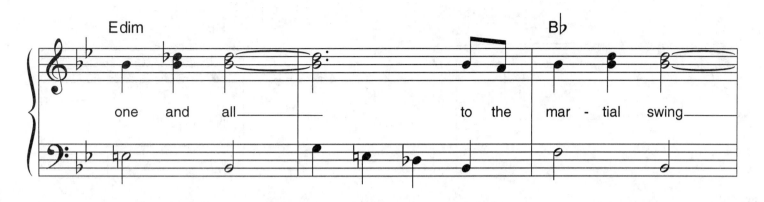

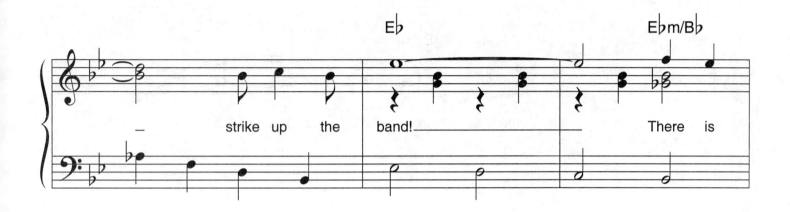

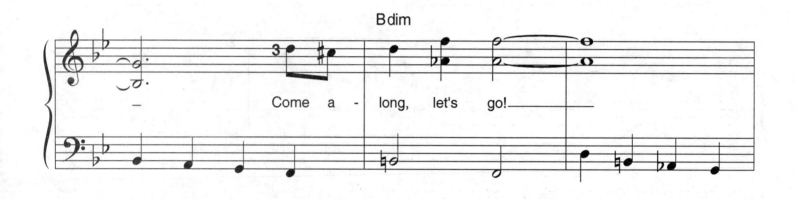

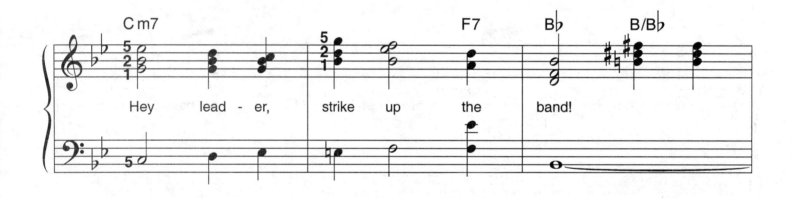

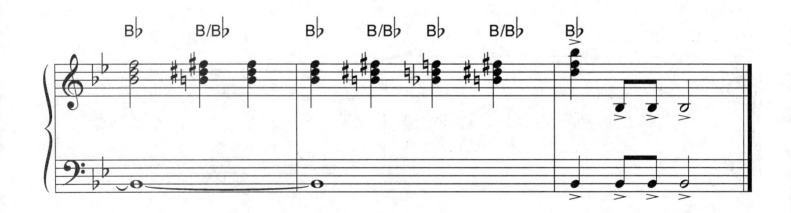

# IF MY FRIENDS COULD SEE ME NOW!

From the Broadway Musical *Sweet Charity*

Music by CY COLEMAN
Words by DOROTHY FIELDS
*Arranged by Richard Bradley*

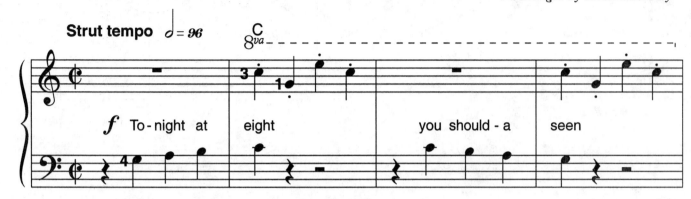

To-night at eight you should-a seen

a chauf-feur pull up in a rent-ed lim-ou-sine!

My neigh-bors burned! They like to die!

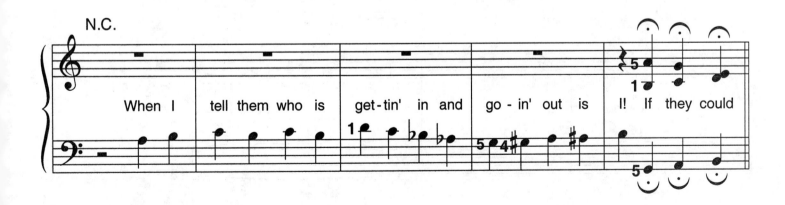

When I tell them who is get-tin' in and go-in' out is I! If they could

*If My Friends Could See Me Now! - 3 - 1*

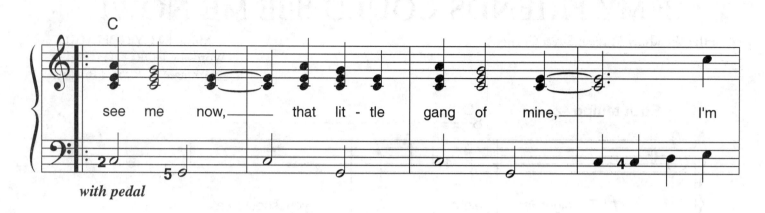

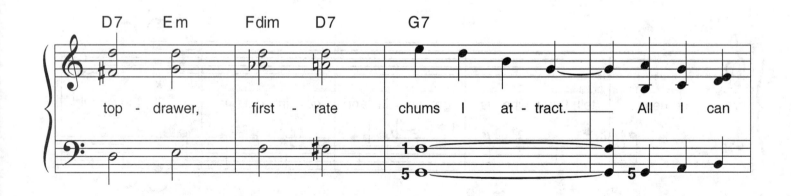

**Verse 2:**
If they could see me now,
My little dusty group,
Traipsin' 'round this
Million dollar chicken coop.
I'd hear those thrift shop cats say:
"Brother get her!
Draped on a bedspread
Made of three kinds of fur."
All I can say is, "Wow!
Wait till the riff and raff
See just exactly how
He signed his autograph."
What a build up! Holy cow!
They'd never believe it,
If my friends could see me now!

**Verse 3:**
If they could see me now,
Alone with Mister V.,
Who's waitin' on me
Like he was a maitre d'.
I hear my buddies saying:
"Crazy, what gives?
Tonight she's living like the other half lives."
To think the highest brow,
Which I must say is he,
Should pick the lowest brow,
Which there's no doubt is me.
What a step up! Holy cow!
They's never believe it,
If my friends could see me now!

# REAL LIVE GIRL

From the Broadway Musical *Little Me*

Music by CY COLEMAN
Lyrics by CAROLYN LEIGH
*Arranged by Richard Bradley*

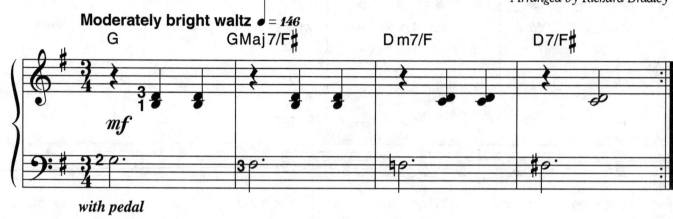

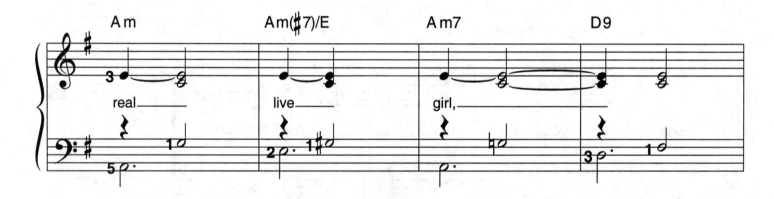

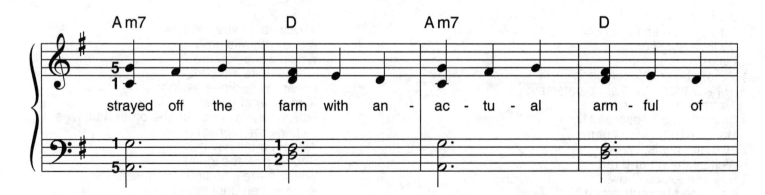

Real Live Girl - 4 - 1

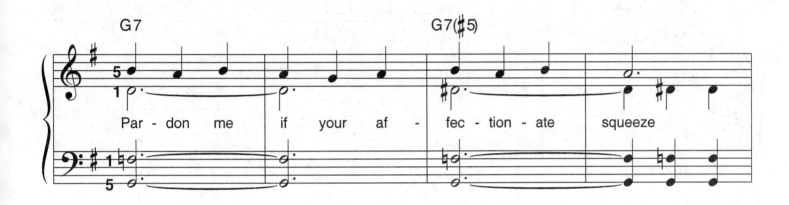

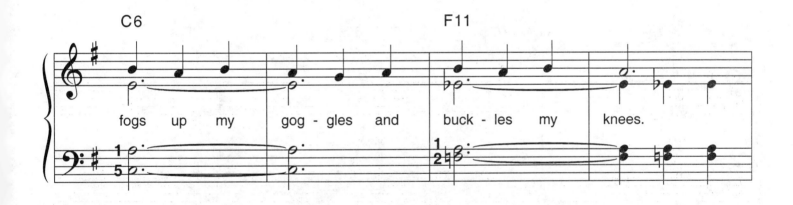

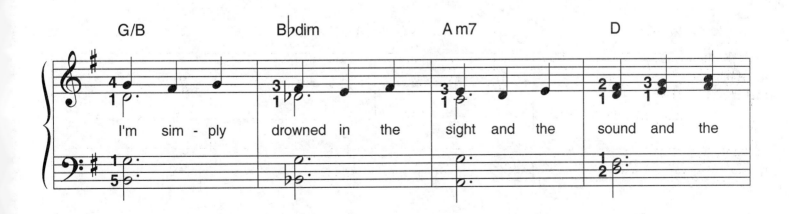

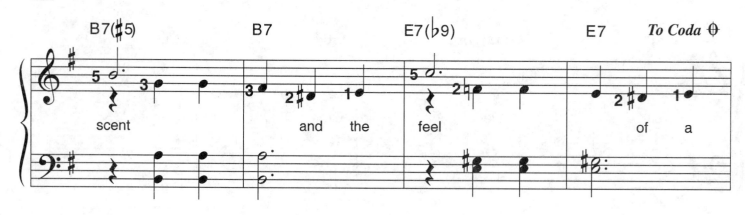

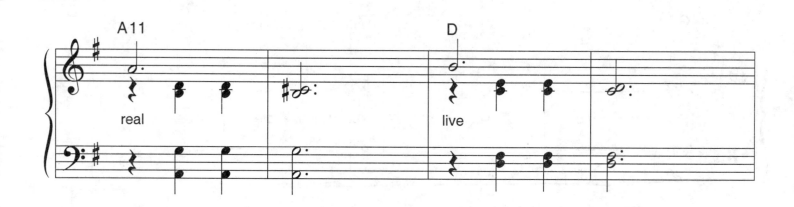

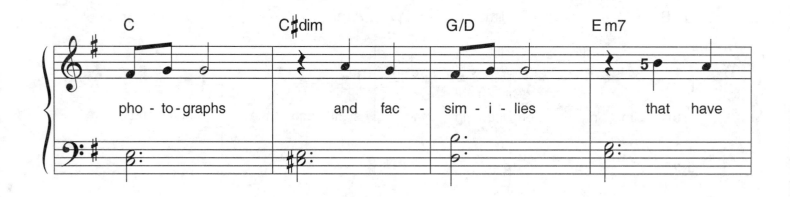

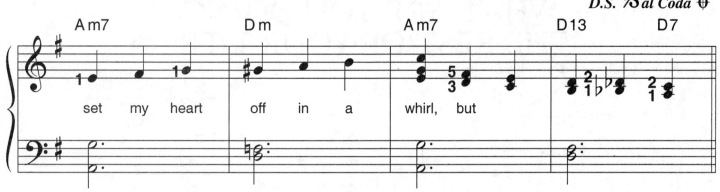

set my heart | off in a | whirl, but

*Coda*
⊕

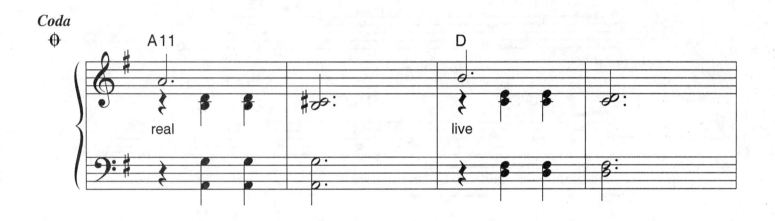

real | live

girl.

*Verse 2:*
Nothing can beat getting swept off your feet by a real live girl.
Dreams in your bunk don't compare with a hunk of a real live girl.
Speaking of miracles, this must be it,
Just when I started to learn how to knit.
I'm all in stitches from finding what riches a waltz can reveal
With a real live girl.

# WHAT ARE YOU DOING THE REST OF YOUR LIFE?

From the Motion Picture *The Happy Ending*

Lyric by ALAN and MARILYN BERGMAN
Music by MICHEL LEGRAND
*Arranged by Richard Bradley*

Lyrics:
What are you do-ing the rest of your life?
North and south and east and west of your life?
I have on-ly one re-quest of your life:
that you spend it all with me:
All the sea-sons and the

*What Are You Doing The Rest Of Your Life? - 4 - 1*

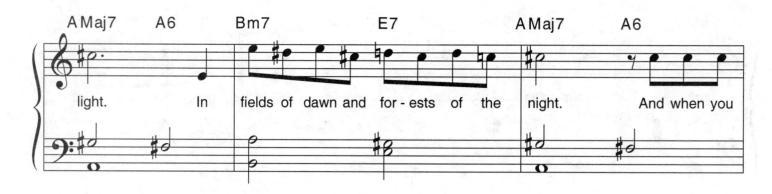

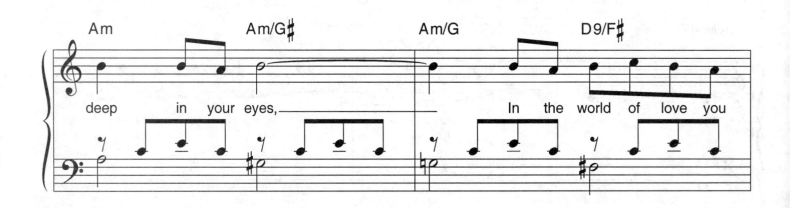

# EMBRACEABLE YOU

From the Broadway Musicals *Girl Crazy* and *Crazy For You*

Words by IRA GERSHWIN
Music by GEORGE GERSHWIN
Arranged by Richard Bradley

Embraceable You - 2 - 1

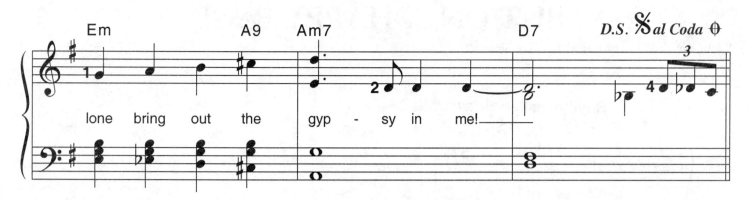

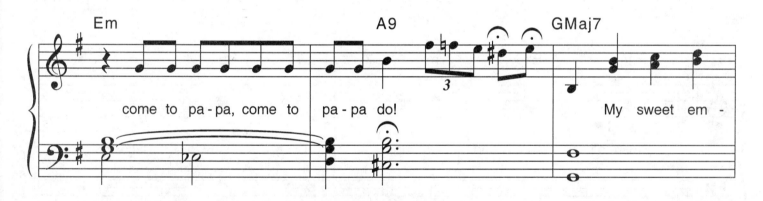

# PUT ON A HAPPY FACE

From the Broadway Musical *Bye Bye Birdie*

Lyrics by LEE ADAMS
Music by CHARLES STROUSE
*Arranged by Richard Bradley*

Put On A Happy Face - 2 - 1

Put On A Happy Face - 2 - 2

# 'S WONDERFUL

From the Broadway Musical *Funny Face*

Words by IRA GERSHWIN
Music by GEORGE GERSHWIN
*Arranged by Richard Bradley*

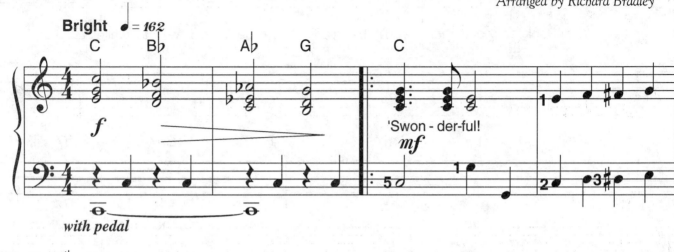

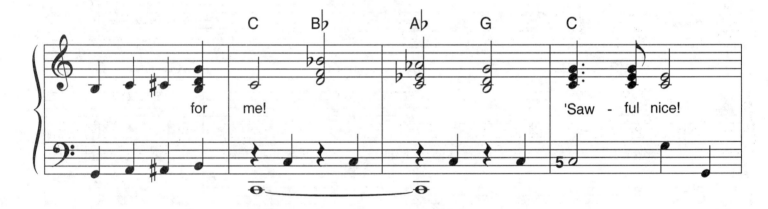

'S Wonderful - 3 - 1

'Smar - vel - ous! That you should

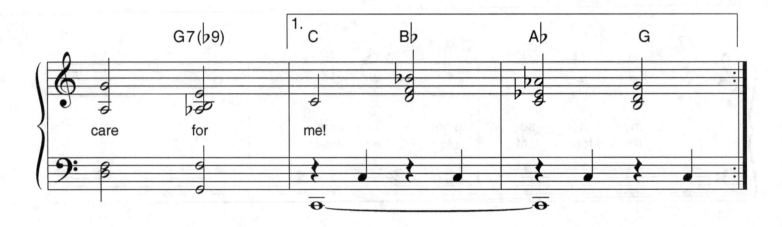

care for me! That you should

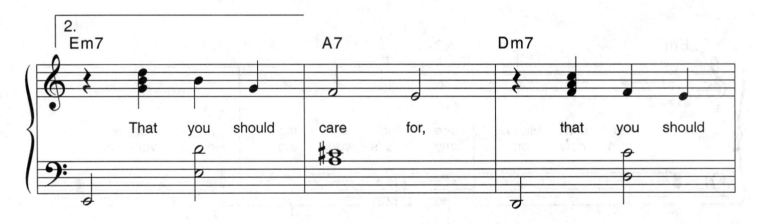

That you should care for, that you should

care for me!

# LOVE AND MARRIAGE

Words by
SAMMY CAHN

Music by
JAMES VAN HEUSEN
*Arranged by Richard Bradley*

Love And Marriage - 3 - 1

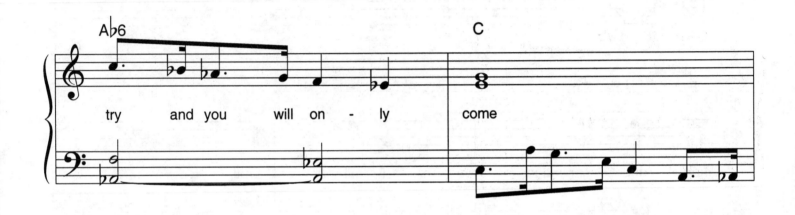

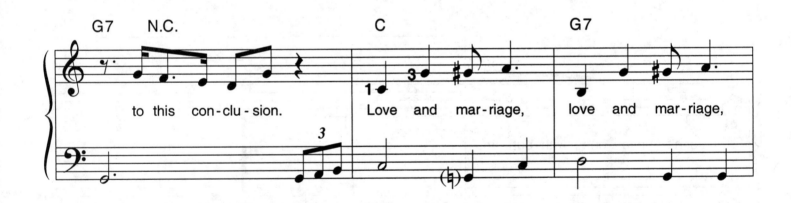

*Verse 2:*
Love and marriage,
Love and marriage,
It's an institute you can't disparage,
Ask the local gentry
And they will say it's elementary.

# THE SECOND TIME AROUND

From the Motion Picture *The Second Time Around*

Words by SAMMY CAHN
Music by JAMES VAN HEUSEN
*Arranged by Richard Bradley*

Love is love-li-er the sec-ond time a-round,_____ just as

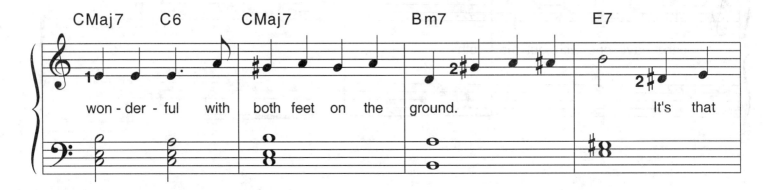

won-der-ful with both feet on the ground. It's that

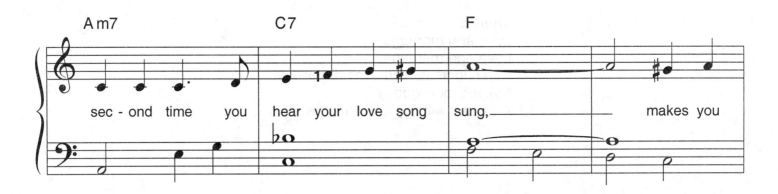

sec-ond time you hear your love song sung,_____ makes you

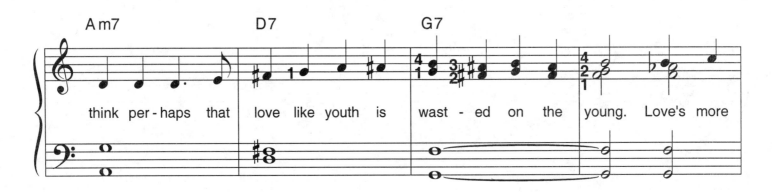

think per-haps that love like youth is wast-ed on the young. Love's more

The Second Time Around - 2 - 1

The Second Time Around - 2 - 2

# WITHOUT YOU

By
WILLIAM HAM and TOM EVANS
*Arranged by Richard Bradley*

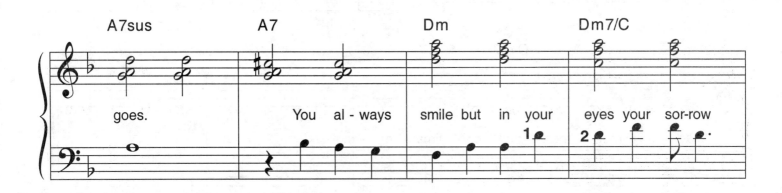

Without You - 4 - 1

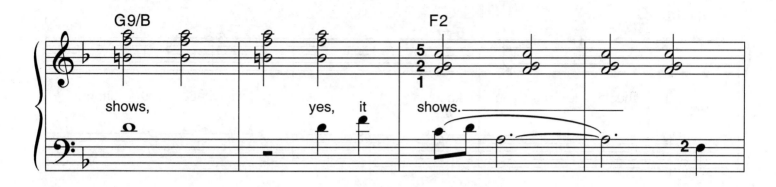

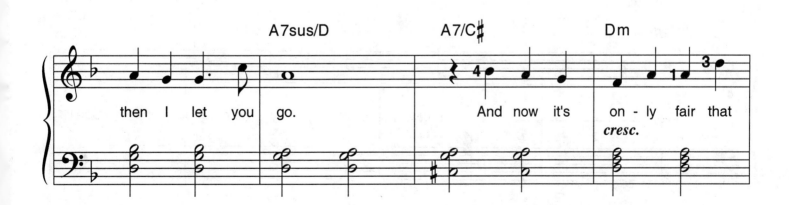

Verse 2:
Well, I can't forget this evening,
Or your face as you were leaving
But I guess that's just the way the story goes.
You always smile
But in your eyes your sorrow shows,
Yes it shows.

# THE MAN I LOVE

From the Broadway Musical *Strike Up The Band*

Words by IRA GERSHWIN
Muisc by GEORGE GERSHWIN
*Arranged by Richard Bradley*

The Man I Love - 3 - 1

236

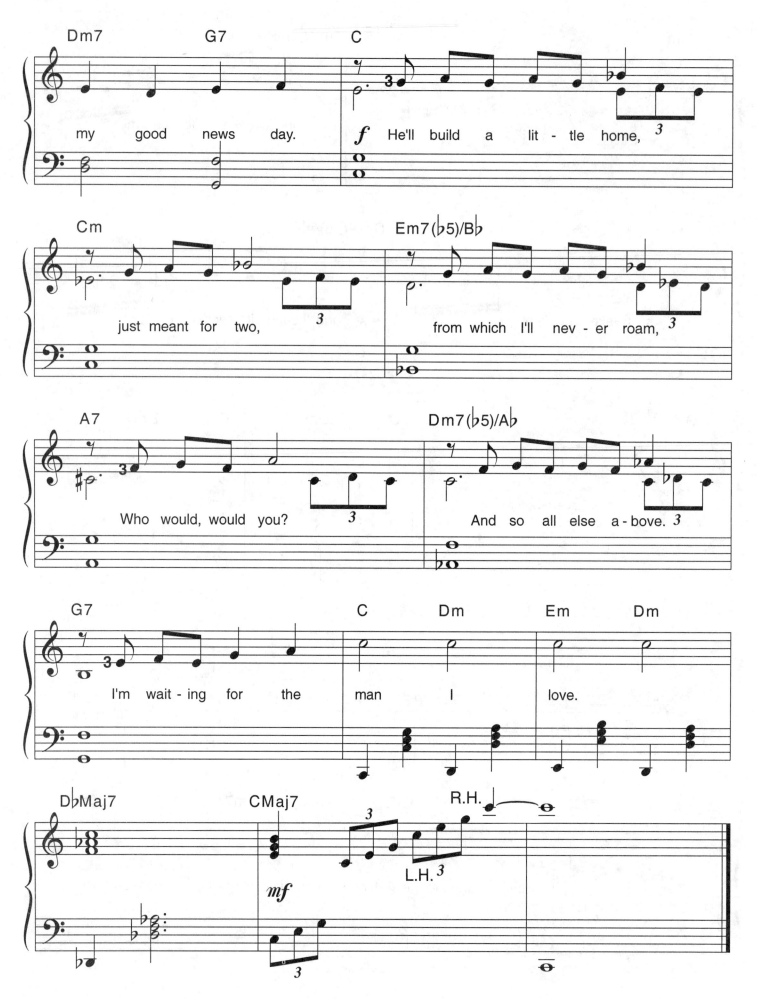

# DON'T GET AROUND MUCH ANYMORE

Lyric by
BOB RUSSELL

Music by
DUKE ELLINGTON
*Arranged by Richard Bradley*

Don't Get Around Much Anymore - 3 - 1

# ARTHUR'S THEME
## (THE BEST THAT YOU CAN DO)

From the Motion Picture *Arthur*

Words and Music by BURT BACHARACH, CAROL BAYER SAGER,
CHRISTOPHER CROSS and PETER ALLEN
*Arranged by Richard Bradley*

Once in your life,___ you'll find her, some-one who turns___ your

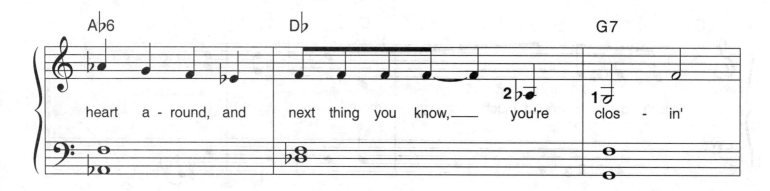

heart a-round, and next thing you know,___ you're clos-in'

Arthur's Theme - 4 - 1

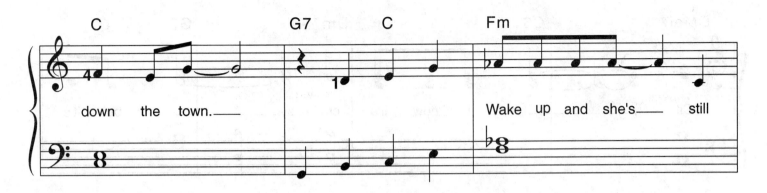

down the town.___ Wake up and she's___ still

with you, e - ven though you left her way a - cross town. You're

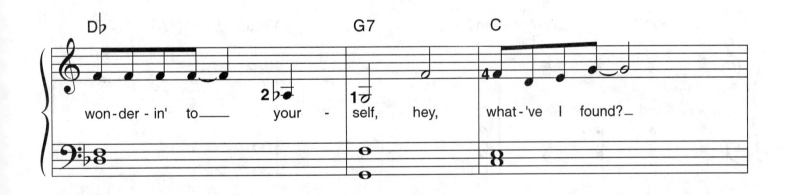

won - der - in' to___ your - self, hey, what - 've I found?___

When you get caught___ be - tween the moon and New York

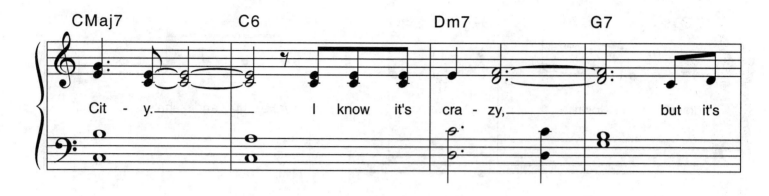

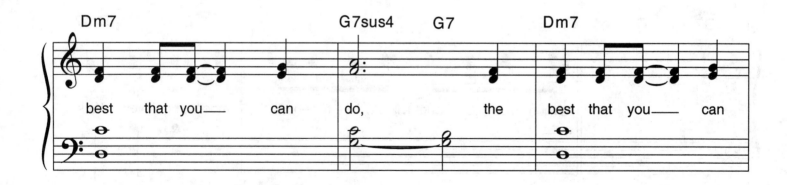

*Verse 2:*
Arthur he does what he pleases.
All of his life his master's toys,
And deep in his heart, he's just,
He's just a boy.
Livin' his life one day at a time
He's showing himself a really good time.
He's laughin' about the way they want him to be.

# I'M THRU WITH LOVE

Words by
GUS KAHN

Music by
MATT MALNECK and FUD LIVINGSTON
*Arranged by Richard Bradley*

I'm Thru With Love - 4 - 1

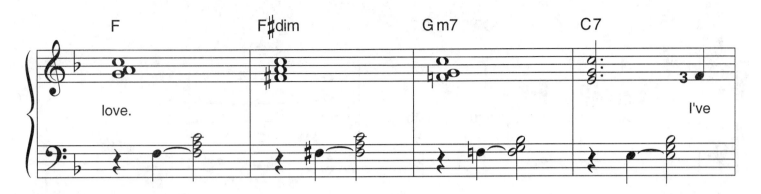

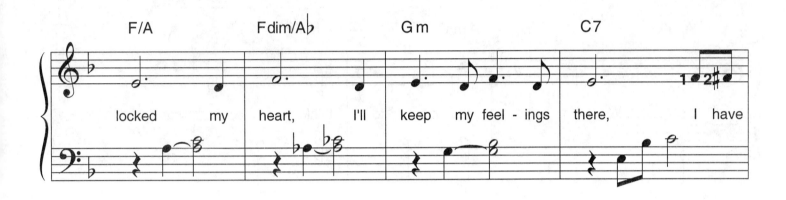

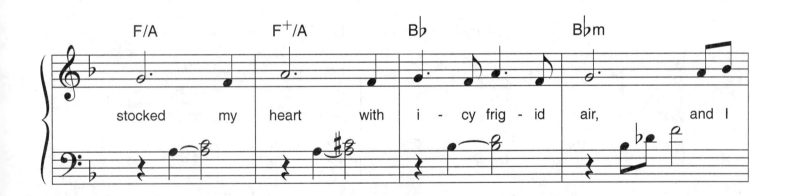

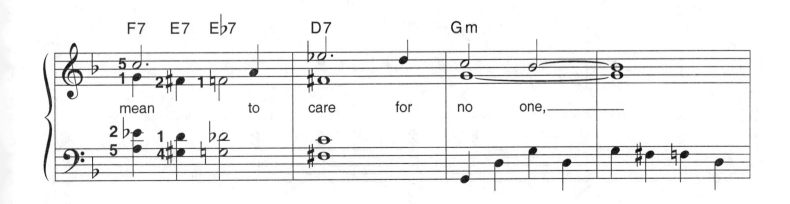

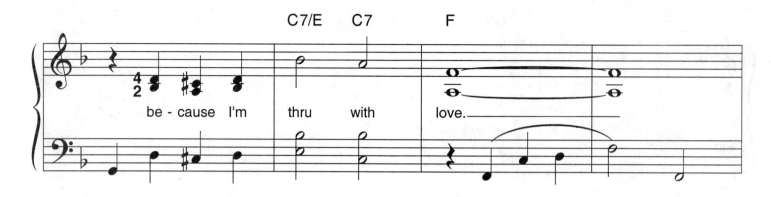

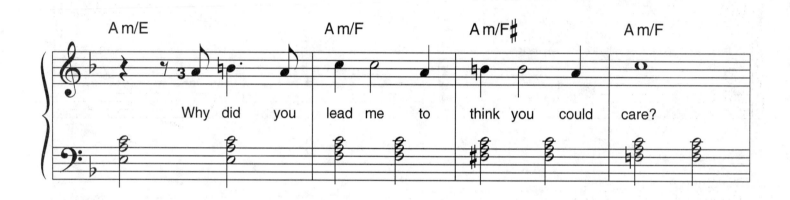

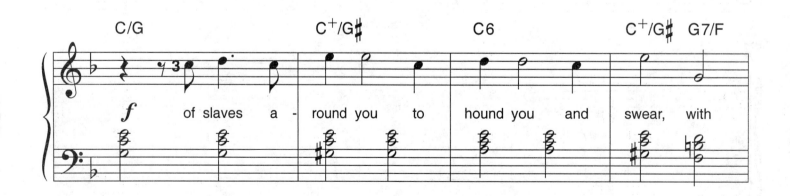

# FRIENDLY PERSUASION
## (THEE I LOVE)

From the Motion Picture *Friendly Persuasion*

Lyrics by PAUL FRANCIS WEBSTER
Music by DIMITRI TIOMKIN
*Arranged by Richard Bradley*

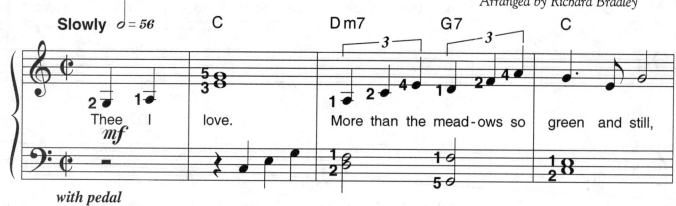

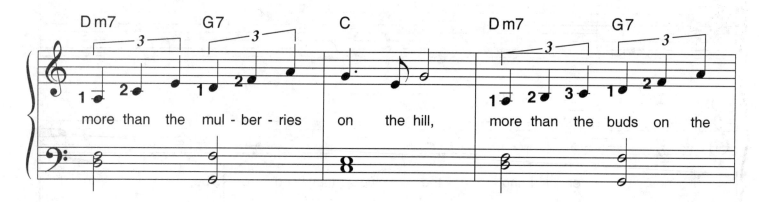

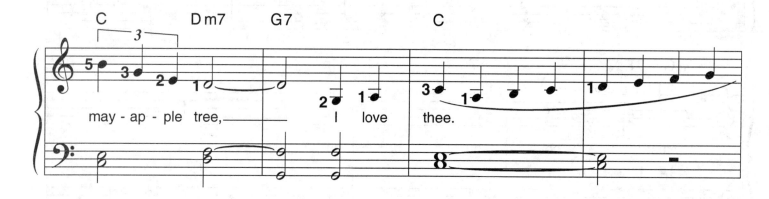

Friendly Persuasion - 2 - 1

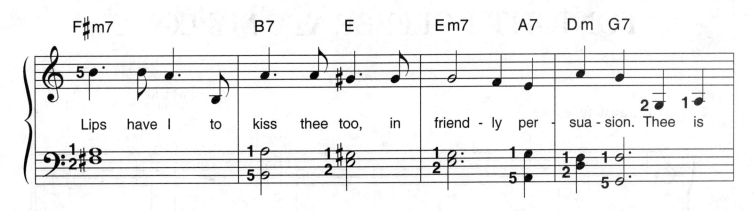

# TONIGHT I CELEBRATE MY LOVE

By
MICHAEL MASSER
and GERRY GOFFIN
*Arranged by Richard Bradley*

Tonight I Celebrate My Love - 4 - 1

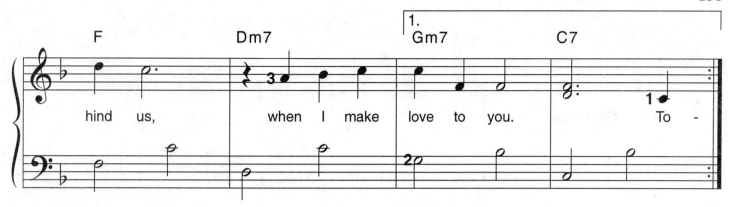

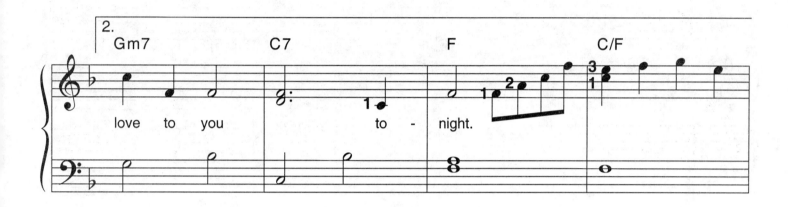

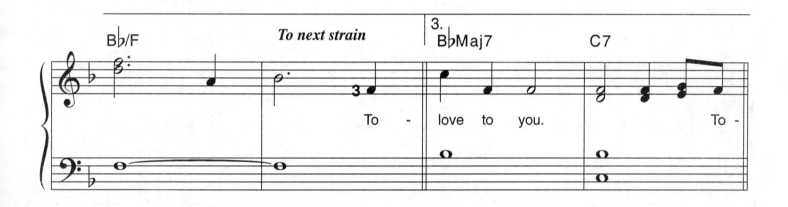

Tonight I Celebrate My Love - 4 - 2

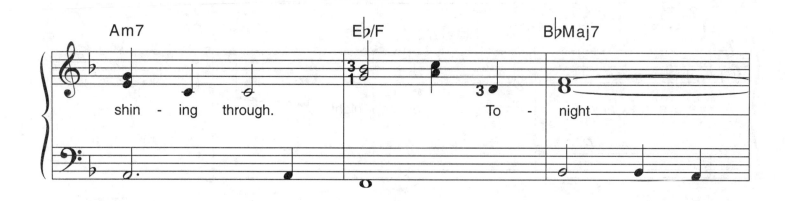

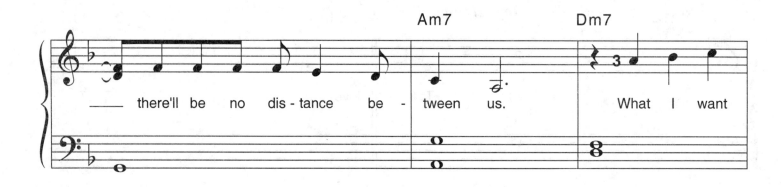

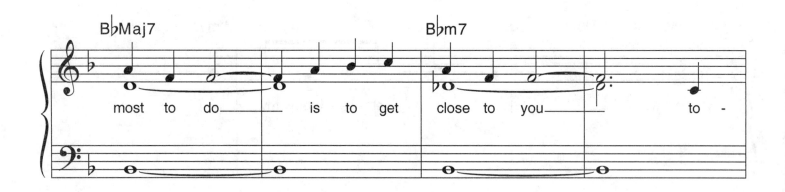

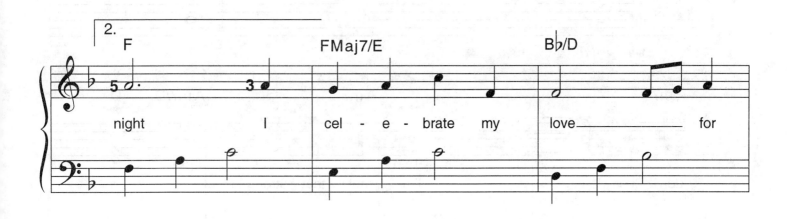

*Verse 2:*
Tonight I celebrate my love for you;
And hope that deep inside you feel it too.
Tonight our spirits will be climbing
To a sky lit up with diamonds
When I make love to you tonight.

*Verse 3*:
Tonight I celebrate my love for you.
And soon this old world will seem brand new,
Tonight we will both discover
How friends turn into lovers,
When I make love to you.

# I WON'T LAST A DAY WITHOUT YOU

Lyrics by PAUL WILLIAMS
Music by ROGER NICHOLS
*Arranged by Richard Bradley*

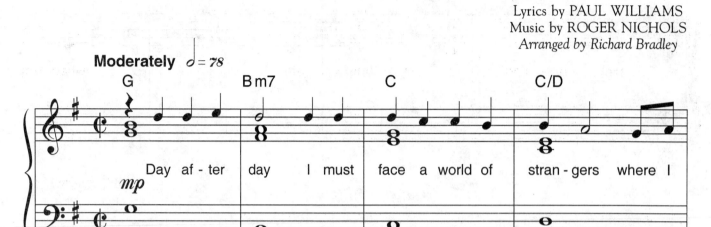

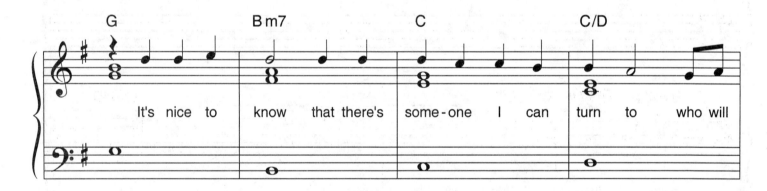

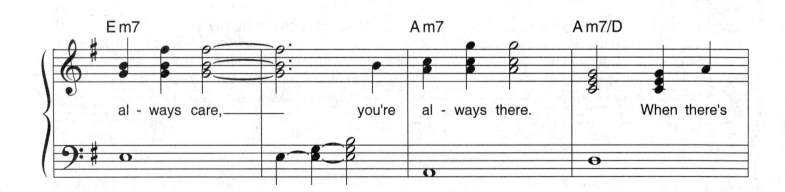

I Won't Last A Day Without You - 3 - 2

Verse 2:
So many times when the city seems to be there
Without a friendly face, a lonely place.
It's nice to know that you'll be there if I need you,
And you'll always smile it's all worth while.

I Won't Last A Day Without You - 3 - 3